Wilfrid Meynell

Cardinal Newman

A Monograph

Wilfrid Meynell

Cardinal Newman
A Monograph

ISBN/EAN: 9783743337428

Manufactured in Europe, USA, Canada, Australia, Japa

Cover: Foto ©ninafisch / pixelio.de

Manufactured and distributed by brebook publishing software (www.brebook.com)

Wilfrid Meynell

Cardinal Newman

THE ILLUSTRATIONS.

1. HIS LAST RESTING-PLACE AT REDNAL.
   (From a Photograph by Mr. MOWLL.)

2. ORIEL COLLEGE, OXFORD.

3. CHURCH OF ST. MARY THE VIRGIN, OXFORD.

4. A SKETCH FROM ST. MARY'S, 1840. (By an UNDERGRADUATE.)

5. THE MONASTERY AT LITTLEMORE.

6. J. H. NEWMAN IN 1844. (From the Portrait by G. RICHMOND, R.A. By permission of Mr. M'LEAN.)

7. THE CHURCH OF THE LONDON ORATORY.
   (From the Drawing by Mr. GRIBBLE.)

8. THE HOUSE OF THE BIRMINGHAM ORATORY.
   (From a Photograph by Mr. MOWLL.)

9. INTERIOR OF THE CHURCH OF THE BIRMINGHAM ORATORY. (From a Photograph by Mr. MOWLL.)

10. CARDINAL NEWMAN IN 1880. (From the Portrait by Sir J. E. MILLAIS, R.A. By permission of Messrs. AGNEW.)

11. FAC-SIMILE OF "LEAD, KINDLY LIGHT."
    (By permission of the owner, the Rev. Dr. G. F. LEE.)

12. A LAST PORTRAIT (on the Cover).
    (From a Photograph by Father ANTHONY POLLEN.)

DEDICATION.

To the Very Rev. WILLIAM LOCKHART,
Of the Institute of Charity.

My dear Father Lockhart,

Your secession from the Church of England, while you were under Dr. Newman's care at Littlemore, was the immediate cause of his resignation of his pastorate at St. Mary's. You, then, had the glory of leading, and he the glory of following where you led. When one remembers what small causes bring large results, it is worth while to record that you yourself owed your conversion to a chance encounter with a book in the keeping of an undergraduate of St. John's College—now known as Father Ignatius Grant, S.J. That book was Milner's "End of Controversy," and it was the beginning of the end of Controversy for you.

So, in linking your name with that of Cardinal Newman, I am only recalling a passage in the personal history of the great Oxford Movement towards the Church of the Apostles. I hope you will think I can with equal fitness associate your dear and honoured name with any publication of mine; since it was under the cover of your friendship, fifteen years ago, that my first scribbler's tasks were taken in hand. Allow me, then, to offer this public expression of gratitude and of love to one who has done favours to so many and is by many so greatly loved.

I am, my dear Father Lockhart,
Always affectionately yours,
"JOHN OLDCASTLE."

AUTHOR'S PREFACE.

My intention, in beginning this record, was to get together scattered records of Cardinal Newman already published by friends in various volumes not all of them accessible to all; adding to these such new facts and anecdotes as other old friends, still surviving, could supply. I had mentally sketched out a history of the places most closely associated with him—some of them already places of pilgrimage—and for the whole collection I thought of the name "Newmaniana."

But before I came to the end of it, this history of his habitations had grown into a Monograph. In speaking of the place I had told of the man who made it memorable while the association lasted. Anecdotes and reminiscences wove themselves into the text; and I found that I had made a sort of *mémoire pour servir*. Cardinal Newman has written his own mental and spiritual autobiography in the "Apologia"; and the completeness of his performance covers the ground, once for all; which is perhaps why we have as yet no announcement from the Birmingham Oratory (though Father Ryder, most fitting of biographers, is there) of an official "Life" of the Cardinal—only the notice of a collection of letters.

For the moment, therefore, these pages may be welcome to some as containing the completest record yet made of the movements and surroundings of Cardinal Newman all his life long. I hasten to add my grateful acknowledgments to those to whom alone that completeness is due: the friends and companions of the Cardinal who have given me their aid: chief among them all, the Rev. Frederick S. Bowles, who was his disciple at Littlemore, who was received into the Church with him, who went with him to Maryvale, to Cotton Hall, and finally to Birmingham, where he remained with him as a Father of the Oratory for many years.

PALACE COURT, LONDON, W.
September, 1890.

HIS LAST RESTING-PLACE AT REDNAL.

(THE CENTRE GRAVE OF THE THREE GRAVES IN A LINE TOGETHER IS THAT OF CARDINAL NEWMAN.)

CHAPTER I.

THE NEWMAN FAMILY.

The Cardinal's Father—The Doubtful Rewards of Industry—An Unsuccessful Career—The Promise of its Fruits—"A Mother of Men"—Family Verses—Studious Sisters—The One Young Dead of a Long-lived Family—Frank Newman and a Growing Asunder—Charles Newman and a Swift Division—Uneventful Youth—Brief and Various Homes—A Note of Later Abiding-places—Travelling with Pre-occupations—Hither and Thither in the Years to Come.

JUDAS, though generally assigned another profession, was undoubtedly a banker—he "kept the purse." But banking, in modern England at any rate, has come to be associated with philanthropy and piety, generally with Evangelicalism. Three of the most illustrious converts to the Catholic Church in the early middle of this century were sons of men connected with London banks—Manning, Newman, Ward. Brewers also, by some freak of restitutional justice, are men mostly given to good works—out of the brewery. Cardinal Newman's father first banked, then brewed, and failed at both. It was not that he allowed his Freemasonry, or his music, or his scheme for the reafforesting of England, to distract him from business; for after the bank in Lombard Street broke during a financial crisis, he became the slave of his brewery at Alton—to no purpose. There is something melancholy in the picture of the man who deserves, but does not command, success; nor does Cato's encouragement avail him. What real comfort Mr. John Newman had, he had from his son, John Henry, who was able to give him the good news of his election to a Fellowship at Oriel in 1823. The father died soon afterwards, a man disappointed in himself, and not realising the greatness which awaited the son who bore his name. He was a Cambridge man by birth. The family had

2

been small proprietors of land; but it was Newman's want of "high connexions" that placed the aristocratic Pusey at the nominal head of the Oxford Movement towards the bark of the Fisherman built by the Carpenter's Foster-Son.

Jemima Fourdrinier, when she married John Newman in 1800, brought her husband a small fortune, which, after the bank and brewery went, was all that remained for the family to live upon, until John Henry's earnings swelled the slender purse. Of Huguenot descent, and belonging to a family of famous paper-makers, whose plate still appears on Ludgate Hill, she was a woman of sound sense and of personal piety—Calvinistically tinged. Misfortune she took kindly: also her son's Catholi-cising mission. This had not gone very far when she died, in the spring of 1836; the Oxford Movement being then only three years old. Ten years earlier, John Henry had written of her in some verses addressed to his brother, "F. W. N.," on his twenty-first birthday:

> My brother, 'tis no recent tie
>   Which binds our fates in one,
> E'en from our tenderest infancy
>   The twisted thread was spun;
> Her deed, who stored in her fond mind
> Our forms, by sacred love enshrined.
>
> In her affection all had share,
>   All six, she loved them all;
> Yet on her early-chosen pair
>   Did her full favour fall;
> And we became her dearest theme,
> Her waking thought, her nightly dream.
>
> Ah! brother, shall we e'er forget
>   Her love, her care, her zeal?
> We cannot pay the countless debt,
>   But we must ever feel;
> For through her earnestness were shed
> Prayer-purchased blessings on our head.
>
> Though in the end of days she stood,
>   And pain and weakness came,
> Her force of thought was unsubdued,
>   Her fire of love the same;
> And e'en when memory fail'd its part,
> We still kept lodgment in her heart.

And when her Maker from the thrall
  Of flesh her spirit freed,
Nor suffering 'companied the call,
  —In mercy 'twas decreed—
One moment here, the next she trod
The viewless mansion of her God.

Now then at length she is at rest,
  And, after many a woe,
Rejoices in that Saviour blest,
  Who was her hope below ;
Kept till the day when He shall own
His Saints before His Father's throne.

So it is left for us to prove
  Her prayers were not in vain ;
And that God's grace-according love
  Has fall'n as gentle rain,
Which, sent in the due vernal hour,
Tints the young leaf, perfumes the flower.

In the Anglican church at Littlemore which Newman built, with the funds of Oriel, he placed a tablet to the memory of his mother, who died just before its consecration.

The six children were equally divided as to sex ; and the names of the three girls were Harriett, Jemima, and Mary. Harriett, the eldest, married in September, 1836, the Rev. Thomas Mozley, then already the brilliant Boswell of the future Cardinal. Before she died, Mrs. Thomas Mozley made two appearances as the author of children's stories, "The Fairy Bower" and "The Lost Brooch." Jemima married Mr. John Mozley, of Derby, in the spring of 1836 ; outlived her husband ; and died, in Derby, about ten years before the death of the Cardinal. Yet another of the Mozley brothers, the Rev. Dr. James Mozley had in 1832 described his future sisters-in-law in a letter home : "The Miss Newmans are very learned persons, deeply read in ecclesiastical history, and in all the old divines, both High Church and Puritanical. Notwithstanding—[O why "notwithstanding"?]—they are very agreeable and unaffected." These two sisters were hero-worshippers, and John Henry was the hero. They looked after his poor at Littlemore, and they gave him what he had the grace to thank God for

                A countless store
          Of eager smiles at home.

The family circle had been lessened so early as in 1828 by the death of the third and youngest girl. What Charlotte Brontë says in poignant words of her sister Emily may be said again: "Never in all her life had she lingered over any task that lay before her, and she did not linger now. She sank rapidly. She made haste to leave us." In apparently perfect health one noon, by the next noon Mary Newman was gone. Pusey's thoughts turned affectionately to his friend in this hour of grief, almost of panic. "Every consolation," he wrote, "which a brother can have he has most richly—her whole life having been a preparation for that hour." Other "Consolations in Bereavement" had Newman, and he thus expressed them:

> Death was full urgent with thee, sister dear,
>   And startling in his speed;
> Brief pain, then languor till thy end came near—
>   Such was the path decreed,
>   The hurried road
> To lead thy soul from earth to thine own God's abode.
>
> Death wrought with thee, sweet maid, impatiently:
>   Yet merciful the haste
> That baffles sickness;—dearest, thou didst die,
>   Thou wast not made to taste
>   Death's bitterness,
> Decline's slow-wasting charm, or fever's fierce distress.
>
> Death wrought in mystery; both complaint and cure
>   To human skill unknown:—
> God put aside all means, to make us sure
>   It was His deed alone;
>   Lest we should lay
> Reproach on our poor selves that thou wast caught away.
>
> Death came and went:—that so thy image might
>   Our yearning hearts possess,
> Associate with all pleasant thoughts and bright,
>   With youth and loveliness,
>   Sorrow can claim,
> Mary, nor lot nor part in thy soft soothing name.
>
> Joy of sad hearts and light of downcast eyes!
>   Dearest, thou art enshrined
> In all thy fragrance in our memories;
>   For we must ever find
>   Bare thought of thee
> Freshen this weary life, while weary life shall be.

To both of his brothers, John Henry was able to be a benefactor, in part a father: a noble and common rôle which ought before now to have given elder brothers a larger place among the heroes of romance. Francis William, only four years younger, followed him to school at Ealing, and then to Oxford, where he lived for some time in lodgings, pursuing his studies under John Henry's directions. Already the difference of temperament was marked, though in religion Frank was then an Evangelical, John Henry not much more. But, even so, Frank thought him wanting in sympathy with his Evangelical friends, so did not consult him about his own difficulties. But Frank himself! A master of style, he made his words fit his strange fancies about the Catholic religion; they were as arrows poisoned by his prejudices. John Henry, a little later, in what he thought a particularly Apostolic mood, would not speak to Frank, whom he had shortly before invoked in fraternal rhymes :

> Dear Frank, we both are summoned now,
> As champions of the Lord;
> Enrolled am I; and shortly thou
> Must buckle on the sword;
> A high employ, nor lightly given,
> To serve as messengers of Heaven.

The season of silence passed away. The difference grew greater, but with a difference—they agreed to differ. They met from time to time, in after years, Frank visiting his brother at Maryvale (where spirits were high); at Rednal; and in Birmingham. Writing to Mr. Lilly in 1877, Dr. Newman, as he then was, says : " The *Dublin* has a practice of always calling me *F.* Newman, whereas my brother is commonly distinguished from me by this initial, his name being Francis. I say this because, much as we love each other, neither would like to be mistaken for the other." Nor was there much fear. Francis William Newman, deist, vegetarian, anti-vaccinationist, to whom a monastery is even as a madhouse, and a nun a woman beside herself, had an utterance too distinct in its idiosyncrasy to be any but his own : and has it still—sole left of all his name.

It remains to speak of the least spoken-of member of the family, he of whom the Rev. Thomas Mozley ventures only : " There was also another brother, not without his share in the heritage of natural gifts." Charles Robert Newman, before he was out of his teens, decided that his brothers and sisters were too religious for him ; and he wrote to cousins, begging that he should no longer be thought of as a Newman: a vain desire, for only as such is he remembered now. His mother was still alive, and she and his sisters tried to win him, but without success, from the life of loneliness and isolation he elected to lead. Never was a kindness denied him, however one-sided the arrangement might be. Both his brothers, after they had been "cast off" by him, not he by them, managed to put together funds for sending him to take a degree at Bonn University, at his earnest desire. But he came away without even offering himself for examination, a step he explained by saying that the judges would not grant him a degree because of the offence he had given by his treatment of faith and morals in an essay which they called *teterrima*. This was only one of a series of aids given to Charles by John Henry and by Francis, who, unlike in so much, resembled each other in their generous desires and actions towards their mother's youngest son. But in him they found, as one of them expresses it in a private letter, only "the closest representation of an ancient cynic philosopher this nineteenth century can afford." He had vicissitudes of fortune; and fortune was never much kinder than to afford him an ushership in a country school; a post it was not in his character to keep. For the last forty years of his life, which ended in 1884, he lived at Tenby; and there, two years before he died, he had a short visit from the Cardinal—at the very time when "Lead, kindly Light," was being sung at Christ Church round Pusey's open grave.

Born in the City of London in 1801, and spending his first years within a mile or two of the Mansion House, John Henry Newman did not go further afield than to Ealing for his first venture in the great world. From Dr. Nicholas's school he went straight to Trinity College, Oxford. Almost immediately afterwards the Newman family removed to Alton, and stayed there for two or three years, during which time John Henry spent his holidays there, delighting in White's "Natural History of Selborne," a few miles away. Other holidays in those earlier days of his Oxford life he spent with the Rev. Samuel Rickards, at Ulcombe, in Kent, or at Stowlangloft, near Bury St. Edmunds. In 1827 he and his sisters paid a visit to Mr. Wilberforce, at Highwood; where three out of the four sons were to be among his followers to Rome. His holidays were his season of verse-making. At Ulcombe he wrote "Nature and Art" in 1826, and "Snap-dragon" (a Trinity memory) in 1827. At Highwood he wrote "The Trance of Time." At Strand-on-the-Green the Newmans settled for a short time. In 1829, all who were left of them at home—the mother and two girls—went to a cottage at Horspath, to be near John Henry; then to a cottage at Nuneham Courtney, offered to Newman by Dornford, a Fellow of Oriel. "In the Midlands," says Thomas Mozley, "it would have been set down as the habitation of a family of weavers or stockingers." But it had its associations. Rousseau had stayed in it; and Nuneham was supposed to be Goldsmith's Deserted Village. From Nuneham to Rosebank Cottage, Iffley, was no great move; and it was the last the family made.

In their wanderings during the earlier twenties of the century the Newmans lived a while at Brighton. There he wrote his "Paraphrase of Isaiah, chap. lxiv.," the second piece of his "Verses on Various Occasions," in 1821. Six years later and eight years later he visited it again to see cousins, in one of whose albums he wrote verses on each visit—his "Opusculum" in 1829. At Brighton, too, when his mother and sisters had left it for the neighbourhood of Oxford, Newman landed after the journey with Hurrell Froude to the south of Europe. The MS. of "Lead, kindly Light," written on the voyage, was in his pocket; and he was hurrying home, inspired by the conviction that he had "a work to do in England," arriving just in time to hear Keble preach that sermon on the Sunday in July, 1833, which began the Oxford Movement. His life had been despaired of for a week in Sicily. He was in a high fever, and no medical help was at hand. A priest came and offered his services, which were declined. In his half-delirious caprice he got up and walked for some miles. Then he sank down exhausted, and was carried into a hovel, which a doctor chanced to pass, to whose care Newman owed, under God, his recovery. At Lyons he fell ill again; his legs and ankles swelled—he thought with erysipelas. All this time—six weeks —his friends at home heard nothing of him, and were horribly anxious. When he landed in Brighton, having crossed from Dieppe, he still felt a little weakness lingering from the fever; but he looked much better than when he set out, partly, perhaps, because his face was well tanned by exposure to the sun.* To Brighton the Cardinal went again after another notable journey. This was on his return to England after visiting Rome in 1879 to receive his Cardinal's hat. On this journey, too, it had seemed that he must die; but the time had not yet come, though he had done the work he felt he had to do when he set foot there nearly fifty years before. In the morning of the last

* What was Newman to his valet?—the Neapolitan servant to whom he said, sitting on his bed and crying in Sicily: "I shall not die, for I have not sinned against light. I have a work to do in England." This servant came to England with Newman, and was afterwards engaged by Lord Carrington.

Sunday in June, 1879, accompanied by Father Neville, he went to the Church of St. John the Baptist, where he was received at the door by Fathers Johnson and Sammons, and where he assisted at High Mass—for the first time in this country as a Cardinal. In the afternoon he drove to the other Catholic churches in the town, and visited the clergy attached to them. The bells of Anglican steeples rang out early in the morning, as only High Churchmen make them ring, and all the day; but not invitingly for him, albeit he was, as the *Guardian* candidly expressed it when he died, " the founder of the Anglican Church as it now is."

CHAPTER II.

AT TRINITY AND ORIEL.

Degree—The Scholar of Trinity—" Trinity had never been unkind to me"—Departure—A Trinity Sunday in After Life—A Trinity Friend—Fellow of Oriel—The First of Pusey and of Keble—Diffidences—Ordination—The First Publicities of Pulpit and Pen—"I began to be known"—The University Pulpit—A Group of Great Listeners—Profound Memories—Newman in his Habit as he Lived—Word Portraits—A Prophet's Chamber—A Neighbour at Oriel.

AT Trinity College Newman took his degree in 1820, and he remained there for three years longer in the coveted position of Scholar. For this home of the first six years of his Oxford life he ever retained the tenderest affection. There he had the dreams of his lay life; there he moulded what was afterwards matured. When he left Oxford "for good," as he himself phrased it with perhaps a double meaning in the words, one of his friends who came to Littlemore to say good-bye was Dr. Ogle, who had been his private tutor at Trinity. " In him," he says, " I took leave of my first college, Trinity, which was so dear to me, and which held in its foundation so many who had been kind to me both when I was a boy, and all through my Oxford life. Trinity had never been unkind to me. There used to be much snap-dragon growing on the walls opposite my freshman's rooms there, and I had for years taken it as the emblem of my own perpetual residence even unto death in my University." At distant intervals during the next thirty-two years a traveller to and from Birmingham looked from the railway carriage, with feelings his fellows could not have divined, at the spires of Oxford; but he did not revisit it until 1878. Trinity attracted him there again, having elected him in 1877 an Honorary Fellow. He was the hero of cheering undergraduates; and he attended the College "gaudy" in the glare of limelight : fêted for the first time in his already long life.

The feelings he all along entertained for his old haunt had been expressed ten years earlier in a letter, dated from Birmingham, Trinity Monday, 1868, and addressed to the Rev. Thomas Short, of Trinity:

My dear Short,—It is fifty years to-day since I was elected scholar of Trinity. And, as you had so much to do with the election, I consider you my first benefactor at Oxford. In memory of it I have been saying Mass for you this morning. I should not have ventured to write to tell you this; but, happening to mention it to William Neville, he said, "Do write and tell him so, for I said Mass for him yesterday, being

ORIEL COLLEGE, OXFORD.

J. H. NEWMAN ELECTED FELLOW IN 1823.

Trinity Sunday." This letter will at least show the love we bear to you and old Trinity amid all changes. Take it as such, and believe me to be, affectionately yours,

JOHN H. NEWMAN.

The Cardinal, visiting Oxford in 1878 and 1880, called on Mr. Short, who had then become blind, and spent an hour with him. He called also on Dr. Pusey; and Mark Pattison, who had, by then, drifted far from the old moorings he held to, when a guest at Littlemore, in 1843.

After Trinity, Oriel seemed strange to Newman, when, in 1823, he was elected to a Fellowship there. "During the first years of my residence at Oriel," he himself says, "though proud of my College, I was not quite at home there. I was very much alone, and I used often to take my daily walk by myself." On one such occasion he met Dr. Copleston, then Provost, who turned round, made him a bow, and said : "Never less alone than when alone." At first he had no friend but Pusey ; and even to Pusey, though Newman "could not fail to revere a soul so devoted to the cause of religion, so full of good works, so faithful in his affections," he could not open his heart —then or afterwards. Keble, too, was a Fellow of Oriel, and when Newman, newly-elected, went to receive the congratulations of the Fellows, he bore it all until Keble took his hand ; and then, he says : "I felt so abashed and unworthy of the honour done me, that I seemed desirous of quite sinking into the ground." But Keble was not in residence ; and was shy of him, so Newman thought, in consequence of the marks the newcomer still bore of the Evangelical and Liberal schools. Hurrell Froude, quoting the murderer who had done one good thing in his life, boasted of himself only that he had brought Newman and Keble finally "to understand each other" in 1828. As time went on things wonderfully changed. By 1824 Newman took orders and was appointed curate at St. Clement's ; he preached his first University sermon ; became a tutor of his College, and a public examiner; and wrote one or two essays which were well received. "I began to be known." He had for his intimate friends Hurrell Froude and Robert Isaac Wilberforce, afterwards the fellow-Archdeacon of Manning in secession to Rome. His hold on young men began. It was a grip of goodness ; an attraction which was not of earth—at a time when an attraction of the kind was a new and a wondrous thing. This influence was widely extended in 1828, when Newman became Vicar of St. Mary the Virgin—a post involving no change of residence, but gaining for him the ear of the University. He had for his listeners the future clergy of the Church of England, of all schools, and not these only. In no other case quite so much expert and other testimony has been given to the influence of spoken words—as regards both the words themselves and the way they were spoken. That other great figure in the history of the revival of the Catholic Church in England forms a fitting first witness ; for Cardinal Manning recalls even now, after a lapse of sixty years, being led captive by the "form and voice and penetrating words at Evensong in the University Church," where, having once seen and heard Newman, he "never willingly failed to be." Dean Stanley—no name follows Manning's as so great a contrast—agreed in this:

There are hardly any passages in English literature [he says]

ST. MARY THE VIRGIN, OXFORD.

J. H. NEWMAN APPOINTED VICAR IN 1828.

which have exceeded in beauty the description of music, in his University sermons; the description of the sorrows of human life in his sermon on the pool of Bethesda; the description of Elijah on Mount Horeb; or, again, in the discourses addressed to mixed congregations:

"The Arrival of St. Peter as a Missionary in Rome;" the description of Dives as the example of a self-indulgent voluptuary; the account of the Agony in the Garden of Gethsemane, and of the growth in the belief in the Assumption of the Virgin Mary.

Among his listeners was one who was already studying the mechanism of oratory:

Now, Dr. Newman's manner in the pulpit, says Mr. Gladstone, was one about which, if you considered it in its separate parts, you would arrive at very unsatisfactory conclusions. There was not very much change in the inflexion of the voice; action there was none. His sermons were read, and his eyes were always bent on his book, and all that, you will say, is against efficiency in preaching. Yes, but you take the man as a whole, and there was a stamp and a seal upon him; there was a solemn sweetness and music in the tone; there was a completeness in the figure, taken together with the tone and with the manner, which made even his delivery, such as I have described it, singularly attractive.

Principal Shairp put into words the thoughts of many hearts when he said: "On those calm Sunday afternoons he was heard preaching from the pulpit of St. Mary's, 'As if the angels and the dead were his audience.' That voice it was which thrilled young hearts—that living presence that drew to itself whatever there was in Oxford that was noble in purpose, or high and chivalrous in devotion." "No one," says Mr. James Anthony Froude, "who heard his sermons in those days can forget them:"

They were seldom directly theological. Newman, taking some Scripture character for a text, spoke to us about ourselves, our temptations, our experiences. His illustrations were inexhaustible. He seemed to be addressing the most secret consciousness of each of us—as the eyes of a portrait appear to look at every person in the room. They appeared to me to be the outcome of continued meditation upon his fellow-creatures and their position in the world, their awful responsibilities, the mystery of their nature, strangely mixed of good and evil, of strength and weakness. A tone, not of fear, but of infinite pity, ran through them all.

It was in St. Mary's that men learned how to bear great names greatly; like Lord Coleridge, who then founded the opinion he expressed in later years: "Raffaelle is said to have thanked God that he had lived in the days of Michael Angelo; there are scores of men I know, there are hundreds and thousands I believe, who thank God that they have lived in the days of John Henry Newman." The voice is silent for ever now; but the printed words remain; and these in bare type retain their hold. Mr. R. H. Hutton* confesses that the University sermons, and other works, have "fascinated" him ever since he was eighteen or nineteen; and he adds: " I have often said that if it were ever my hard lot to suffer solitary confinement, and I were given my choice of books, and were limited to one or two, I should prefer some of Dr. Newman's to Shakspere himself." A little incident, or a large one—who shall reckon?—brought him down from that pulpit in 1843—two years before his secession: the beginning of the great Renunciation. " It was," says Principal Shairp, " as when to one kneeling by night, in the silence of some vast Cathedral, the great bell tolling solemnly overhead has suddenly gone still."

The young generation does not associate the name of Cardinal Newman with horses or vintages; but it is Mr. Froude, I think, who somewhere refers to him as the trusted wine-taster of Oriel; and to his love for horse exercise there are many allusions in Mr. Mozley's "Reminiscences." In his earlier Oriel days he rode a good deal. Besides taking his chance of the Oxford hacks, Newman had for some time a pretty, but dangerous animal, Klepper, brought over from Ireland by Lord Abercorn, then at Christchurch.

One little matter of self-imposed duty, arising out of a painful occasion, will, says Mr. Mozley, be remembered by all who ever accompanied Newman in a country walk. One morning Dornford asked him whether he was going to Littlemore that day, and whether on foot or horseback. He had to reply that he was riding there, when Dornford proposed to accompany him. This gentleman, having served two years in the Rifle Brigade in the Peninsular War, and being proud of his military character, was in the habit of cantering on the hard road, and had generally to do it alone. But Newman was in for it. In those days the first milestone between Oxford and Iffley was in a narrow, winding part of the road, between high banks, where nothing could be seen fifty yards ahead. Dornford and Newman heard the sound of a cart, and the latter detected its accelerated pace, but the impetuous 'captain,' as he loved to be styled, heeded it not. It was the business of a cart to keep its own side. They arrived within sight of the cart just in time to see the carter jump down and be caught instantly between the wheel and the milestone, falling dead on the spot. The shock on Dornford was such that he was seriously ill for two months, and hypochondriac for a much longer time. The result in Newman's case was a solemn vow that whenever he met a carter driving without reins, or sitting on the shaft, he

---

[*] " I have now for twenty years held him, as a journalist, to be a good friend of mine," the Cardinal wrote to me in 1884.

would make him get down; and this he never failed to do. Several years after this sad affair, I was walking with him on the same road. There came rattling on two newly-painted waggons, drawn by splendid teams, that had evidently been taking corn to market, and were now returning home without loads. There were several men in the waggons, but no one on foot. It occurred to me that as the waggoners were probably not quite sober, it was only a choice of evils whether they were on foot or in the waggons. But Newman had no choice; he was bound by his vow, and he compelled the men to come down. We went on to Littlemore, were there for some time, and then turned our faces homewards. Coming in sight of the public-house at Littlemore, we saw the two show teams, and something of a throng about them; so we could not but divine evil. It was too true. The waggoners had watched us out of sight, and got into their waggons again. The horses had run away on some alarm, one of the men had jumped out, and had received fatal injuries.

Other examples of the Cardinal's habits of self-discipline at this time are on record. He never passed a day without writing a Latin sentence—either a translation or an original composition—before he had done his morning's work. Frequently, when on the point of leaving his room for an afternoon walk, he has asked a friend to stay a minute or two while he was writing his daily sentence. One more habit, for such it was, is mentioned. As well for present satisfaction as for future use, the Cardinal wrote and laid by a complete history of every serious question in which he was concerned, such as that of the College tuition. He did the same with every book he read and every subject he inquired into. He drew up a summary or an analysis of the matter, or of his own views upon it.

Mr. Mozley's word-portrait of his brother-in-law at this period tallies with the "Sketch from St. Mary's"—from the pencil of an undergraduate:

Newman did not carry his head aloft or make the best use of his height. He did not stoop, but he had a slight bend forwards, owing perhaps to the rapidity of his movements, and to his always talking while he was walking. His gait was that of a man upon serious business bent, and not on a promenade. There was no pride in his port or defiance in his eye. Though it was impossible to see him without interest and something more, he disappointed those who had known him only by name. They who saw for the first time the man whom some warm admirer had described in terms above common eulogy, found him so little like the great Oxford don or future pillar of the Church, that they said he might pass for a Wesleyan minister. John Wesley must have been a much more imposing figure. Robust and ruddy sons of the Church looked on him with condescending pity as a poor fellow whose excessive sympathy, restless energy, and general unfitness for this practical world would soon wreck him. Thin, pale, and with large lustrous eyes ever piercing through this vale of men and things, he hardly seemed made for this world. Canon Bull meeting him one day in the Parks, after hearing he had been unwell, entreated him to spare what fibre he had for a useful career. "No ordinary frame can

A SKETCH FROM ST. MARY'S, 1840.

stand long such work as yours." His dress—it became almost the badge of his followers—was the long-tailed coat, not always very new. There is a strange tendency in religious schools to express themselves in outward forms, often from the merest accident. Newman, however, never studied his "get up," or even thought of it. He had other uses for his income which in these days would have been thought poverty. It became the fashion of the party to despise solemnity of manner and stateliness of gait. Newman walked quick, and, with a congenial com-

At Trinity and Oriel.

panion, talked incessantly. George Ryder said of him that when his mouth was shut it looked as if it never could open; and when it was open it looked as if it never could shut. Yet he was never so busy or so preoccupied but that he had always upon him a burden of conscientious duties to be attended to, calls of civility or kindness, promises to be fulfilled, bits of thoughtfulness to be carried out, rules of his own to be attended to.

Mr. J. A. Froude's description is, perhaps, less trustworthy, because more picturesque:

He was above middle height, slight and spare. His head was large, his face remarkably like that of Julius Cæsar. The forehead, the shape of the ears and nose were almost the same. The lines of the mouth were very peculiar, and I should say exactly the same. In both men there was an original force of character, which refused to be moulded by circumstances, which was to make its own way, and become a power in the world; a clearness of intellectual perception, a disdain for conventionalities, a temper imperious and wilful, but along with it a most attaching gentleness, sweetness, singleness of heart and purpose. Both were formed by Nature to command others; both had the faculty of attracting to themselves the passionate devotion of their friends and followers.

Newman's rooms at Oriel, on the first floor near the chapel, communicated with what was no better than a large closet, overlighted with an immense bay window over the chapel door. It had been a lumber-room; but, says Mozley, "Newman fitted it up as a prophet's chamber, and there, night after night, in the Long Vacation of 1835, offered up prayers for himself and the Church. Returning to College late one night I found that, even in the gateway, I could not only hear the voice of prayer, but could even distinguish words. The result was, Newman contented himself with a less poetical oratory." Strangers coming daily to Oxford, and seeking out the abode of the man who was "moving the Church of England to its foundations," were surprised to find him in simple undergraduate's lodgings. In the rooms above lived William Froude, Hurrell's younger brother, who was to be Brunel's helper in laying out the Bristol and Exeter Railway, and who was to make for himself a more difficult spiritual way to Rome. While Newman was praying, William Froude was making laughing gas and staining his window-sills with sulphuric acid. From 1837 to 1840, Mozley records: "Newman had no College office or work, and was seldom seen in Hall; but he gave receptions every Tuesday evening in the Common Room, largely attended by both the College and the out-College men." He did not resign his Fellowship until October, 1845.

CHAPTER III.

LITTLEMORE.

*Search after Seclusion—Cloister, **Cells**, and Crucifix—Resolution as to his Position—Disciples—Hard Fasting—A Significant Visit—The first to go—Curiosity, and Newman's resentment of it—Father **Dominic receives Newman**—A First and Last **Mass**—A Jesuit's Strange Offer—Primitive Confession—Father Newsham's Laughter—Final **Farewells**.*

NEWMAN had too many visitors in Oriel to be able to give to the Fathers the serious study he felt they demanded; and he withdrew to Littlemore, which lies two or three miles to the south of Oxford, towards London. He had always loved the place, and it had the tradition of being the healthiest spot near about. The parish was included in the pastorate of St. Mary the Virgin; and for many years Newman walked from Oxford to Littlemore two or three times a week. Since he had built the church there, the sound of the stonemason's hammer had not been heard, and he could find nothing better for his new residence than a disused range of stabling at the corner of two roads. Nothing could be more unpromising; but Newman said it was enough; and his handy man was there to help in the work of reconstruction—Thomas Mozley, a master-builder, too, of words, whose "Reminiscences" have again and again helped me in the patchwork of these temporary memoirs. Newman made known his needs. There must be a library, some "cells," and a cloister—the chapel was to be for future consideration. The library was to be the common workroom; and each cell was to contain a sitting-room, say 12 feet by 9 feet, a bedroom 6 feet by 6 feet; the height of both to be 9 or 10 feet. Newman bought nine acres which he proposed to plant with firs, and on which he could build, bit by bit, as the money came and the men. He expressed only one sentimental wish to the reconstructor—that he might be able to see from his own cell window the ruins of the Mynchery—a convent dating from Saxon times, inhabited of old by generations of Benedictine Nuns, and dedicated to "Our Lady of Littlemore." Newman's decision as he paced the cloister, or knelt before the crucifix (for he had ceased to be superstitiously afraid of crucifixes), or studied the Fathers, now was: that he could go on in the University pulpit only on condition that he was allowed to hold by the Catholic interpretation of the Anglican Articles set forth in "Tract XC."; but that he would relapse into lay life in the Church of England rather than join the Church of Rome "while she suffered honours to be paid to the Blessed Virgin and the Saints, which I thought in my conscience to be incompatible with the Supreme, Incommunicable Glory of the One Infinite and Eternal;"* that he desired a union between the Churches, on conditions; that Littlemore was, as he called it, his *Torres Vedras*, and that he and his followers might advance again within the Anglican Church, as they had been forced to retire; and, finally, that he must keep back with all his might intending seceders to Rome. Everything indicated that he came to the village to stay—not to make it, as it turned out to be, his home of only five or six years' duration.

When all was done the place still looked outside what it had always been—a range of stabling. But these were not the times for "externals"; and the cells were soon filled with men all in deadly earnest about "the interior life." "They were most of them," says "the Vicar," as they called him, "keenly religious men, with a true concern for their souls as the first matter of all, with a great zeal for me, but giving little certainty at the time as to which way they would ultimately turn. Some, in the event, have remained firm to Anglicanism, some have become Catholics, and some have found a refuge in Liberalism." Of the latter, one name comes to mind on the moment—that of Mark Pattison. Pattison had his habitation in a sort of Community-house established on Apostolic principles by Pusey in Oxford itself; and he was a guest, not a resident, when he stayed at Littlemore. What attracted the future Rector of Lincoln

* Looking back to those days, after years of experience as a Catholic, he says: "Only this I know full well now, and did not know then, that the Catholic Church allows no image of any sort, material or immaterial, no dogmatic symbol, no rite, no sacrament, no Saint, not even the Blessed Virgin herself, to come between the soul and its Creator. It is face to face, *solus cum solo*, in all matters between man and his God. He alone creates; He alone has redeemed; before His awful eyes we go in death, and in the vision of Him is our eternal beatitude."

College to Tractarianism was "the interest it excited in the young in all religious practices and exercises, and in many religious questions which had been matters of indifference."* Mark Pattison kept a diary during a fortnight's visit to Newman at the close of September, 1843, and these are some of the entries, showing what manner of life Littlemore led:

Newman kinder, but not perfectly so.† Vespers at eight. Compline at nine. How low, mean, selfish my mind has been to-day; all my good deeds vanished; grovelling, sensual, animalist; I am not, indeed, worthy to come under this roof.

Sunday, October 1st.—St. John called me at 5.30, and at six went to Matins, which, with half Lauds and Prime, takes about an hour and a-half; afterwards returned to my room and prayed, with some effect, I think. Tierce at nine, and at eleven to church—communion. More attentive and devout than I have been for some time; thirty-seven communicants. Returned and had breakfast. Had some discomfort at waiting for food so long. Walked up and down with St. John in the garden; Newman afterwards joined us; and at three to church; then Nones; walked in the garden till dinner—interesting talk. Some unknown benefactor sent a goose. Talk of some Rosminian Nuns coming to England;‡ though an Order, and under the three vows, they do

* Newman somewhere says that his old friends were distressed to see him surrounded in the early 'forties by "younger men of a cast of mind in no small degree uncongenial to my own." Some of this was raw material, certainly; and so remained. In after life Mark Pattison wrote: "I am astonished to see what hours I wasted (!) over religious books at a time when I ought to have been devoting every moment to preparation for the Oriel Examination." On a par with this are the reasons he gives for not joining the Catholic Church: "I must have been enveloped in the catastrophe of 1845, as were so many of those with whom I lived, but for two saving circumstances. One of these was my devotion to study. In 1843 Radford offered me a tutorship of the College. My classics had got sadly rusty. I immediately set resolutely to work and made good my lost ground. I think it was chiefly owing to this that when the crash came in 1845 I did not follow Newman." Later on, in his "Memoirs," Mark Pattison, feeling perhaps that everything still remained to be said on this subject, gives another version. He says: "In dealing with the students I soon became aware that I was the possessor of a magnetic influence, which soon gave me a moral ascendancy in the College. In this fact, which was very slowly making itself felt, lies the true secret of my not having followed Newman." When someone compiles, O strangest collection of inadequacies! a volume of men's "Reasons why I did *not* join the Church of Rome," Mark Pattison's will still remain, with Keble's, among the most perplexing.

† Poor Mark Pattison, in his self-torturing sensitiveness, had supposed, "up to 1838 the only sentiment Newman can have entertained towards me was one of antipathy."

‡ The future Rosminian, Father Lockhart, was *not* at the dinner-table. He had gone on pilgrimage to the shrines of St. Gilbert of Sempringham; and on the journey he joined the Catholic Church.

not renounce possessions in the world. They aim to embrace the whole Church. The Jesuits always and everywhere opposed and despised; St. Ignatius prayed for this; Wiseman opposed the Jesuits at Rome, and does so here; proof of his sincerity. Vespers at eight, Compline at nine. Very sleepy, and went to bed at ten.

October 3rd.—Lockhart's mother much distressed. Probably at the separation, more than at the conversion, which she must have expected some time.

October 4th.—N—— mentioned to me having just received the account of a lady who, having in conversation declared she thought the Church of Rome the true Church, had been refused the Communion by her minister, he telling her in so many words to go to Rome.

October 5th.—Coffin came to-day to stay. How uncomfortable have I made myself all this evening by a childish fancy that once got into my head—a weak jealousy of N——'s good opinion. Oh! my God, take from me this petty pride! Coffin more subdued and less thoughtless than usual.

This particular way of introducing the name of Coffin will perhaps a little surprise those afterwards acquainted with the ascetic Provincial of the English Redemptorists, who took on himself, when at the end of his life, the burden of the Bishopric of Southwark. Other men of Littlemore, belonging to the group who became Catholics, were Frederick S. Bowles, now Chaplain to the Dominican Nuns at Harrow; John B. Dalgairns, afterwards a London Oratorian, a man of whom Mozley says, "I feel sure he might have taken his place among the most popular and instructive writers of the age, and become a household word in England;" "dear Ambrose St. John," the "link between the old life and the new," who lived with Newman as a fellow-priest at the Birmingham Oratory, and now lies with him in one grave at Rednal; Albany Christie, now a Jesuit, who was studying medicine in London with as many interludes at Littlemore as he could get; Brydges, of Merton, whose brother George, and his cousin Matthew, became Catholics too; Richard Stanton, now an Oratorian in London; and Lockhart, the first to go.

If Lockhart's mother was distressed—his master was so too. Speaking of his young men, and of this young man, Newman said: "Their friends besought me to quiet them if I could. Some of them came to live with me at Littlemore. They were laymen or in the place of laymen. I kept some of them back for several years from being received into the Catholic Church. The immediate cause of my resigning St. Mary's was the unexpected conversion of one of them." This was Lockhart; who, after confessing to Newman one day, asked: "But are you sure you have the power of absolution?" "Why will you ask me that question?" replied Newman—" ask Pusey." To Pusey the Littlemorians always supposed that "the Vicar" himself went; so that Pusey could now at least aver that Newman had this much belief in the absolving power of the Anglican clergy. But Lockhart did not trouble Pusey with his question. He went to Father Gentili, whom he had lately met with the De Lisles at Ward's rooms in Oxford; and at the end of a three days' retreat was a Catholic and a Postulant with the Rosminians. Rosmini's "Maxims of Perfection" had been given to him four years earlier by a friend—now Sir William White, our Ambassador at Constantinople; and one of the counsels on which he opened in a moment of hesitation decided him that his duty was to submit there and then to the Catholic Church, despite the promise Newman had extorted from him to linger for three years longer. Father Lockhart, looking back at those days, said in a lecture delivered in St. Etheldreda's, Ely Place, just after Newman's death:

> In speaking of Cardinal Newman and his work, he should necessarily speak of himself, though he spoke of himself only as a type of the ordinary young Oxford man who came fifty years ago under the great Cardinal's influence. To put into one sentence what struck him as the character of his whole teaching and influence, it was to make them use their reasoning powers, to seek after the last satisfactory reason one could reach of everything, and this led them to the last reason of all, and they formed a religious personal belief in God the Creator, our Lord and Master. This was the first thing that Newman did for those young men under his care. He rooted in their hearts and minds a personal conviction of the living God. And he for one could say he never had had that feeling of God before he was brought into contact with Cardinal Newman. Who that had experience of it could forget Newman's majestic countenance—the meekness, the humility, the purity of a virgin heart "in work and will," as the poet says, a purity that was expressed in his eyes, his kindness, the sweetness of his voice, his winning smile, his caressing way, which had in it nothing of softness, but which you felt was a communication to you of strength from a strong soul—a thing to be felt in order to be realised. It was when Newman read the Scriptures from the lectern in St. Mary's Church at Oxford that one felt more than ever that his words were those of a seer who saw God and the things of God. Many men were impressive readers, but they did not reach the soul. They played on the senses and im-

agination, they were good actors, they did not forget themselves, and one did not forget them. But Newman had the power of so impressing the soul as to efface himself; you thought only of the majestic soul that saw God. It was God speaking to you as He speaks to you through creation; but in a deeper way, by the articulate voice of man made to the image of God and raised to His likeness by grace, communicating to your intelligence and sense and imagination, by words which were the signs of ideas, a transcript of the work and private thoughts that were in God. . . . Hearing of Newman's intention to open a place at Littlemore he volunteered to join him, and was accepted. He was one of the first inmates of that home. Newman rooted theism most deeply in their souls, and from that they were led on to the practice of submission and of that religion which they doubted not had come from God, for they had no doubt whatever that the Church of England was a part of that world-wide religious society which Christ had established in the beginning, and which He sent down His Apostles to establish in every land. It was only after beginning to put in practice what Newman had taught them—to go into the last reason of things, which they did step by step, in many cases quite independently of their teacher, because he became a Catholic two years before Newman—that they arrived at that conclusion which he himself reached a little later. Newman was much hurt for his leaving him. But the first step that Newman took after he had become a Catholic was to pay him a visit at the College at which he was then studying. He need not say how happy that day was when he found himself and his old friend once more in the same communion.

After preaching his last sermon as an Anglican in September, 1843, Newman remained two years longer at Littlemore— making sure that he was not doing anything in a hurry. "It is," he says, "because the Bishops still go on charging against me, though I have quite given up: it is that secret misgiving of heart which tells me that they do well, for I have neither lot nor part with them; this it is which weighs me down." And he adds a smaller grief, but a real grievance: " I cannot walk into or out of my house, but curious eyes are upon me. Why will you not let me die in peace? Wounded brutes creep into some hole to die in, and no one grudges it them. Let me alone, I shall not trouble you long." One day, when he entered the house, he found a flight of undergraduates inside. Heads of houses, as mounted patrols, walked their horses round the poor cottages; Doctors of Divinity dived into the recesses of that private tenement uninvited. When the Warden of Wadham, a flourishing Evangelical, knocked one day at the door, Newman opened it himself:—nothing so human as a housemaid entered the "monastery," where the inmates took the duty of door-opening for a week by turns. " May I see the monastery ? " insinuated the visitor. "We have no monasteries here," replied Newman, and closed the door in his face—less than civil! Then the newspapers had their paragraphs, inviting episcopal attention. So the Bishop of Oxford writes, a little timidly, to ask what it all means :—Is there really an intention to found—he can hardly bring himself to write the naughty word Canon Farrar and all of them have now so glibly at the tongue's end—an Anglican monastery? Newman replies :

For many years, at least thirteen, I have wished to give myself to a life of greater religious regularity than I have hitherto led; but it is very unpleasant to confess such a wish even to my Bishop. I feel it very cruel, though the parties in fault do not know what they are doing, that very sacred matters between me and my conscience are made a matter of public talk. As to the quotation from the newspaper, your Lordship will perceive that "no monastery is in process of erection;" there is no "chapel," no "refectory," hardly a dining-room or parlour. The "cloisters" are my shed connecting the cottages. I do not understand what "cells of dormitories" means. Of course, I can repeat your Lordship's words that "I am not attempting a revival of the Monastic Orders, in anything approaching the Romanist sense of the term."

Rumours flew about; and it was whispered that he "was already in the service of the enemy"—had already been received into the Catholic Church. On the other hand, among Catholics there were murmurs—could he know so much, and yet remain, and be in good faith? What a rebuke to rash judgments it seemed when the Bishop of Clifton recalled them in the presence of the coffin containing all that was mortal of this immortal man! That the resignation of St. Mary's gave him a new sense of freedom may be imagined; and this is, indeed, implied by Newman in the letter he wrote in April, 1845, to Cardinal Wiseman, then Vicar-Apostolic, who had accused him of past coldness in his conduct towards him :

I was at that time in charge of a ministerial office in the English Church, with persons entrusted to me, and a Bishop to obey; how could I write otherwise than I did without violating sacred obligations? . . . If you knew me, you would acquit me, I think, of having ever felt towards your Lordship in an unfriendly spirit, or ever having had a shadow on my mind of what might be called controversial rivalry, or desire of getting the better, or fear lest the world should think I had got the worst, or irritation of any kind. And now in like manner, pray believe, though I cannot explain it to you, that I am encompassed with responsibilities so great and so various as utterly to overcome me unless I have mercy from Him Who, all through my life, has sustained and guided me, and to Whom I can now submit myself, though men of all parties are thinking evil of me.

The story of the life at Littlemore has never yet been told; and it would be impossible to glean from Newman's scanty allusions in the "Apologia," or even from his letter to the Bishop, any idea of its primitive austerities and observances. I tell these as nearly as possible as they are told by Littlemore men to me. Lent was a season of real penance for the inmates. They had nothing to eat each day till five, and then the solitary meal was of salt fish. No wonder Dr. Wootten, the Tractarian doctor, told them they must all die in a few years if things went on so; and no wonder Dalgairns had a serious illness, at which some relaxations were made—a breakfast, of bread and butter and tea, at noon; taken standing up at a board—a real board, erected in the improvised refectory, and called in undertones by some naturally fastidious ones a "trough." The "chapel" was hardly more pretentious than the dining-room. At one end stood a large crucifix, bought at Lima by Mr. Crawley, a Spanish merchant living in Littlemore. It was what was called "very pronounced"—with the all but barbaric realism of Spanish religious art. A table supported the base; and on the table were two candles [always lit at prayer-time by Newman], the light of which was requisite; for Newman had veiled the window and walls with his favourite red hangings. Of an altar there was no pretence; the village church at Littlemore being Newman's own during the first years of his residence there. A board ran up the centre of the chapel, and in a row on either side stood the disciples for the recitation of Divine Office; the "Vicar" standing by himself a little apart. The days and hours of the Catholic Church were duly kept; and the only alteration made in the Office was that Saints were invoked with a modification of Newman's making—the "*Ora pro nobis*" being changed in recitation to "*Oret.*" At Christmas and Easter some white silk was placed behind the crucifix, upon the background of red hangings [those red hangings — almost mauve — reappear at Maryvale and at Edgbaston—horrors!], a symbol and proclamation of Divine grace. Among the visitors to Littlemore, a year before *the* visit, was Father Dominic himself. He came, passing through Oxford, and presented himself at Newman's door as one watching with keen interest Anglican development in Christian doctrine. "A *little more* grace," he said, and then the consummation:—an Italian, new to the English language, must be forgiven the pun. Newman took him to Littlemore Church, and there he fell on his knees—doubtless to pray for the happy issue of these strange workings of Divine grace in the heart of Oxford—in the hearts of the very flower of the University which Protestantism had appropriated, and fenced in, and planted about.*

If, on the night of October 8th, 1845, any dons or proctors were prying round the "monastery" (even Newman could not call it the "parsonage-house" after he had ceased to be the parson), they must have seen a strange sight—a monk indeed! Father Dominic, the Passionist, was that night to find the consummation of those hopes he had held almost from the days when he watched his sheep on the Apennines: those hopes that he might get to Northern Europe and to Protestantism, and preach the full Gospel of Christ. The years passed; and the shepherd lad found himself a priest, and was sent to England—and to Aston in Staffordshire. And now Dalgairns, who had already been received by Father Dominic at Aston, and who had returned to find "the Vicar" at the last gasp of Anglicanism, and Ambrose St. John also reconciled to the Church by Monsignor Brindle at Prior Park, suggested that the Passionist should again visit Littlemore. He came, dripping wet from his journey through torrents of rain. Newman knelt before him. The Father bade the neophyte rise, "conscious," says one of his friends, "of a great miracle of grace." Mr. Oakeley, one of Newman's young disciples, who subsequently exchanged the Anglican ministry for the Catholic priesthood, says:

It was a memorable day, that 9th of October, 1845. The rain came down in torrents, bringing with it the first heavy instalment of autumn's sere and yellow leaves. The wind, like a spent giant, howled forth the expiring notes of its equinoctial fury. The superstitious might have said that the very elements were on the side of Anglicanism—so copiously did they weep, so piteously bemoan, the approaching departure of its great representative. The bell which swung visibly in the turret of the little Gothic church at Littlemore gave that day the usual notice of morning and afternoon prayers; but it came to the ear in that buoyant,

* Father Dawson, as an Irish priest, felt a little strange when he found himself impelled to kneel, years afterwards, in the same place. He did not know he was but doing what Father Dominic had done. Nor did Mr. F. W. Grey, the grandson given by Lord Grey to the Faith, who writes: "Silently we knelt in the deserted temple and prayed that its Lord and Master, banished for three hundred years, might quickly return to it again, and then rose and continued our pilgrimage."

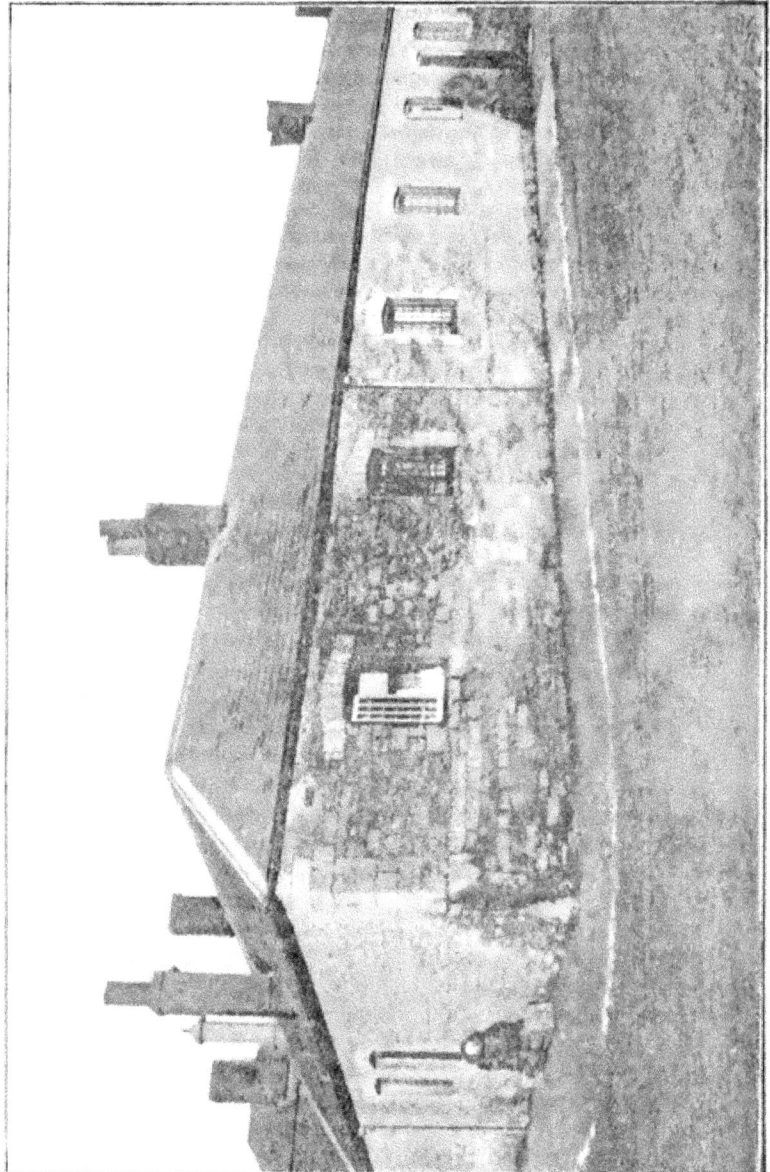

bouncing tone which is usual in a high wind, and sounded like a knell rather than a summons. The monastery was more than usually sombre and still. Egress and ingress there were none that day; for it had been given out, among friends accustomed to visit there, that Mr. Newman "wished to remain quiet." One of these friends, who resided in the neighbourhood, had been used to attend the evening "office" in the oratory of the house, but he was forbidden to come "for two or three days, for reasons which would be explained later." The ninth of the month passed off without producing any satisfaction to the general curiosity. All that transpired was that a remarkable-looking man, evidently a foreigner, and shabbily dressed in black, had asked his way to Mr. Newman's on the day but one before; and the rumour was that he was a Catholic priest. In the course of a day or two the friend before mentioned was re-admitted to the evening office, and found that a change had come over it. The Latin was pronounced for the first time in the Roman way, and the antiphons of Our Lady, which up to that day had always been omitted, came out in their proper place. The friend in question would have asked the reason of these changes, but it was forbidden to speak to any of the Community after night-prayers. Very soon the mystery was cleared up by Mr. Newman and his companions appearing at Mass in the public chapel at Oxford.

Father Dominic, after spending some hours in Newman's "cell," visited Bowles and Stanton. His bow to the Pietà—a German coloured print—as he entered Bowles's room, was a part of his pious simplicity:—Newman said of him he had met no one in whom so much simplicity combined with so much shrewdness; a common Italian type which he must have encountered often enough afterwards. "My dear brother," Father Dominic began to Bowles, "I am surprised that you should dwell in a Church which has no ideas." What followed is hardly remembered now; but need for controversy there was none. The watering and the planting and the grafting (a great deal of that) had been done: now came the harvest. Stanton was a young clergyman, formerly of Brazenose College, and a Hume Exhibitioner, who had resigned his benefice and come to Littlemore. These three, "the Vicar" and the two disciples, entered the curious chapel on Thursday afternoon, October 9th, 1845, and stood in a line together. Function there was none; and Ritualism hid her face. The bowl of Baptism was of domestic, not of ecclesiastical, pattern; and all else was of a tale. Then Father Dominic gave a little address, saying his *Nunc Dimittis*. Dalgairns and St. John went into Oxford, to the primitive Catholic chapel—St. Clement's—and borrowed from the old priest, Father Newsham, an altar-stone and vestments, so that Father Dominic might say Mass the next morning—the first and only time at Littlemore. At that Mass the neophytes received their first Communion. The fervour of Father Dominic, when he made his thanksgiving, greatly impressed the converts, who had not been accustomed in Anglicanism to see so much emotion in prayer. One little incident may be recorded as almost comic. On the evening before their reception into the Church, Father Dominic went into the chapel with the catechumens, and recited Office with them. But when they came to the record of how St. Denis, after his martyrdom, put his head under his arm and walked about, Father Dominic cried "stop," and skipped it over. He thought such legends might be a difficulty to beginners; but he did not know his men; for who was more familiar with miracles and the authority assigned to them than the author of those Essays which had made Macaulay exclaim: "The times require a Middleton?" In truth, the neophytes were rather scandalised at *him*, and not at it.*

Father Dominic left at the end of a three days' visit. As he went back to Oxford he must have recalled a passage in the life of the Founder of the Passionists—St. Paul of the Cross. It tells how he fell into a trance, at the end of which he was asked what vision he had seen, and answered: "O the wonderful works of my children in England!" Confessor and penitent met once again at Maryvale. But the Passionist had done his work. In 1849, he was travelling by rail with one companion, when his mortal illness seized him, and he died upon the platform of Reading Station, blessing England with his latest breath. By some deplorable chance the people who were near, and who might have helped him, feared some infection, and held aloof from him and refused him shelter. Thus died this lover of our country, the humble apostle who reconciled to the Catholic Church him whom her Head afterwards called "the light of England."

For four months after his conversion Newman remained at Littlemore. It was a strange period. The converts went down

---

* Four years later, when the Oratorian Series of Saints' Lives began to be published, the Convert Editors found themselves discountenanced in their love of legend by old Catholics; and the series was temporarily stopped by Newman after it had been accused, in *Dolman's Magazine*, of reducing Hagiology to a string of "unmeaning puerilities." Newman himself hinted afterwards that he had been led into "extravagances" by "younger men."

daily to Oxford to Mass—great curiosities! They found a by-path among fields to escape the public gaze. There is a fine church in Oxford now, and there are Jesuits to man it. But the old St. Clement's was almost comic in its insufficiencies. One announcement made on Sunday was: "Confessions will be heard on Saturday afternoon in the arbour." The arbour in some way communicated with the schoolroom ; and a penitent of the party repairing thither, feeling all the first shyness of a never anything but shy proceeding, found an unexpected embarrassment. Just as the critical moment came, he heard the young barbarians stop their play to listen—"Hush," said the leader, "he's going to begin." There was at least the precedent of the early Church, when Confession was publicly made! Father Newsham walked over to Littlemore; and during his call was perpetually breaking out into ripples of laughter. Newman was a little sore about it—"What did he find so funny about us?" he asked, when the visitor went. The reassuring truth leaked out: the good priest was so overjoyed—he could not contain himself. At last grace had done its work —and he had as his parishioner at St. Clement's the great Mr. Newman of St. Mary's. Other visitors came—among them the Provincial of the Jesuits, with a proposition—astonishing! The Society had a work in hand, and would the converts help in it?— an apostolate in Timbuctoo. Then came partings, the saddest that ever voluntarily were; with Mr. Pattison and Mr. Lewis, both of whom followed Newman to Rome at leisure, and Mr. Church, "Carissime" then, and afterwards as Dean of St. Paul's. "You may think how lonely I am. We are leaving Littlemore, and it is like going on the open sea."*

A dear friend of mine, Father Dawson, O.M.I., during a visit from Ireland to England in 1890 made a pilgrimage to the death-bed of Newman's Anglicanism. Writing of it as it now is, he says in a letter to me : "Yes! that was it—just a little row of one-storey cottages on the side of the village street, and a similar row, joined to it at right angles, running into a lane. The cottages are now in reality separate cottages; but one grave old lady most politely showed me what (as she understood) had been the chapel, the refectory, and the dormitory.

* In the "Apologia," written nearly twenty years later, the Cardinal speaks of spending the last two days at Littlemore " simply by myself "—a slip of memory. Father Bowles was there till the end ; and into his room Newman came each evening, and fell asleep in his chair, worn out with the day's packing. On their last night in Oxford, Newman slept "at my dear friend's, Mr. Johnson's, at the Observatory," as also did Father Bowles.

It looked, indeed, a place of plain living. 'Remember him myself? Oh, yes! I can remember Mr. Newman very well indeed—hearing him preach in the church, and seeing him in the school when I was a little girl. He *was* kind to us, Sir, when he used to come into the school; we were all so fond of him. Ah! what a pity, Sir, he ever left us!' On that point I did not feel willing to dwell, or even to find out for certain whether my venerable hostess meant by 'leaving us' anything besides leaving the village of Littlemore."

JOHN HENRY NEWMAN IN 1844.

(*After a Portrait by* GEORGE RICHMOND, R.A.)

CHAPTER IV.

MARYVALE, ROME, COTTON HALL, AND ALCESTER STREET.

Gives up the idea of a lay life—Confirmed at Oscott—Goes to Maryvale—Two places in a Coach and Five Vans of Books—Studies and Ordination in Rome—" We are to be Oratorians"—Return to Maryvale—Is joined by Faber—Goes to Cotton Hall—A Call to London—The choice of Birmingham—A house in a slum—Cholera duty at Bilston—" Mostly poor and Irish "—Literary and other labour not in vain in the Lord.

AT first Newman had talked of "secular employment"; but Bishop Wiseman knew better. The neophyte came to Oscott, near Birmingham, to be confirmed by the Bishop on November 1st, 1845; together with Oakeley, who had been received into the Church by Father Newsham at Oxford; and Mr. Walker—like his great friend, Stanton, a young ex-clergyman, late of Brazenose, and afterwards a Catholic priest: and while at Oscott, Newman was taken by Wiseman to see a building, then used as a boys' school, near to the College and belonging to it, which he placed at Newman's disposal. " Bring your friends here," said Wiseman, "and carry on your studies for the priesthood, with the help of our professors at Oscott." Newman accepted the house and called it " Maryvale." Thither he went on finally leaving Littlemore, on Monday, February 23rd, 1846; and if any sympathetic fellow-passenger inside the coach which bore Newman and Bowles to Birmingham had suspected that the simply-dressed layman was no other than the late " Vicar " of whom religious England had heard for nearly twenty years, he might, like Wilkie's chance-met travelling companion, have thanked God at finding him so young a man.* Stanton and St. John had gone before

* The portrait by Richmond—a commission from Mr. Henry Wilberforce—best represents Newman at this date. He sat for it in 1844, and the Oratorian collar was substituted for the Anglican minister's tie in the engraving at a later date.

to prepare the house, they having cleverness in such arrangements; and Newman's own furniture and books—especially books—were on the road in five enormous vans.

After a few months at Maryvale, Newman went to Rome, pausing here and there upon the way. The *Univers* of September 20th, 1846, published the following letter from Langres:

The presence of the Rev. J. H. Newman in our city has excited no less interest than it did at Paris. His simplicity and modesty charmed everyone who had the advantage of an admission to his presence. Our venerable Bishop received him with the affection and cordiality of a brother. Forty or fifty members of our clerical body had the honour of being presented to him whose eloquent words affected so lately the studious youth of the principal University of England. The marks of sympathy of which this learned writer was the object have spoken to him of the happiness which Catholics experience in counting him among their brethren. What admirable men are these Oxford converts! God has not without purpose chosen instruments so fitted to accomplish His great designs. Mr. Newman was accompanied by the Rev. Ambrose St. John, who, also, has been admitted to Minor Orders, and repairs to Rome to receive the priesthood. The second companion of Mr. Newman is the Rev. Robert Aston Coffin. Mr. Coffin does not proceed to Rome with his two friends, but returns to England. Mr. Newman and Mr. St. John go from Langres to Besançon. They will travel through Switzerland to Milan, where they remain till they have learnt Italian* before proceeding to Rome. Mr. Dalgairns, who is completing his theological studies at Langres, hopes to return to England next year, where he will await the return from Rome of his friend and instructor.

Of the Archbishop of Besançon, Newman wrote: "He has the reputation and the carriage of a very saintly man." "What you want in England is a strong Bishop," said the Prelate; and Newman, who thought things went a little too easily, agreed. The arrival in Rome is recorded by the Roman Correspondent of the *Daily News*, which had started, under Dickens's editorship, on the very day following Newman's departure from Oxford—an event it did not think worth a mention. The Roman Correspondent—no other than "Father Prout"—says:

On the evening of October 28th Mr. Newman, accompanied by Mr. Ambrose St. John, entered the Eternal City. Next morning the

---

* Newman had learnt some Italian before his tour with Hurrell Froude in 1833, but it was obliterated from his memory during his fever in Sicily; and he afterwards corresponded with his landlord there in Latin.

ex-Anglican proselyte's first impulse was to pay his homage at the Tomb of the Apostles, when, as chance would have it, Pius IX. was in the act of realising Scott's ballad :

> The Pope he was saying his High, High Mass
> All at St. Peter's shrine.

Their interview occurred in the crypt or subterranean sanctuary, the oldest portion of the basilica. It would appear that the inundations of Upper Italy opposed serious obstacles to the progress of the Oxford pilgrims, and that at one passage the cart which bore them, drawn by oxen, was well-nigh swallowed up by the rush of many waters. Safe from these semi-apostolic "perils of the flood," they are now engaged, under the guidance of the most intelligent of their countrymen and co-religionists, in a brief survey of whatever is most remarkable here ; and in a few days Mr. Newman, late of Oxford, and his companions, will take possession of chambers in the College of Propaganda, and enter on a preparatory course previous to re-ordination in the Church of Rome.

Newman received Holy Orders at the hands of Cardinal Franzoni, and, in 1847, he announced, in a letter from Rome to Mr. Hope-Scott, the important plans already made :

> We are to be Oratorians : Monsignor Brunelli went to the Pope about it the day before yesterday—my birthday. The Pope took up the plan most warmly. He wishes us to come here, as many as can, form a house under an experienced Oratorian Father, go through a novitiate, and return. I suppose we shall set up in Birmingham.

By the end of 1847* he was back in London, which he reached on Christmas Eve. He went to Bishop Wiseman, who had now settled in Golden Square as Administrator of the London District; and all at once a great development of his plans was opened out. It happened in this wise. Frederick Faber, the Rector of Elton, who had been Newman's "acolyte" at Oxford, and who had been detained in Anglicanism by Newman's influential persuasions to patience, did not wait many days, once he heard of Newman's submission to the Church, to follow it by his own. Then he drifted to Birmingham, where Father Moore at St. Chad's had received many of the Oxford converts ; and he had already formed himself and the friends who came with him from Elton, into a sort of community in a Birmingham slum, when Newman first came to Maryvale. Faber's offer

---

* The Cardinal Archbishop, in his beautiful elegy on his brother Cardinal, speaks of having met him in Rome in 1848—a mistake of a year in the date.

there and then to place himself and his companions under Newman, was declined; and before long **Faber** found himself and his fellows established at Cotton Hall, near Alton, by the Earl of Shrewsbury, who bought for him a piece of land to build upon beside the Catholic church at Cheadle. Here the "Brothers of the Will of God," or "Wilfridians," grew and prospered for eighteen months, until the time came, in Advent, 1847, when Faber should proceed to London to take the community vows before Bishop Wiseman. Arriving in Golden Square, he found, with Wiseman, Father Stanton, just arrived from Rome—the first wearer of the Oratorian habit in England. "Why not combine?" said Wiseman—a thought which had already taken possession of Father Faber. Why not? The question was repeated to Father Newman, who arrived shortly afterwards, and to whom Faber paid a visit at Maryvale, in January, 1848, when all details were settled.

Next month Father Newman, with Stanton and St. John, visited Faber at Cotton Hall, and formally received Faber and his Wilfridians into the rule of St. Philip Neri. Writing a few days afterwards, Faber said: "Father Superior has now left us, all in our Philippine habits, with turn-down collars, like so many good boys brought in after dinner. In the solemn admission, he gave us a most wonderful address, full of those marvellous pauses. He showed how, in his case and ours, St. Philip seemed to have laid hands upon us, whether we would or not. I hardly know what to do with myself for very happiness." To Maryvale Faber went, with Newman for his novice-master; but he returned to Cotton Hall almost immediately; and his novitiate ending, by dispensation, in July, 1848, he became novice-master there to the new Community. In the month of October in that year, all the Fathers from Maryvale joined their brethren at Cotton Hall, at the instance of Bishop Wiseman. The Community were now forty in number, flourishing exceedingly. The ceremonies of the Church were carefully carried out, and Father Faber had already made some two hundred converts in the neighbourhood. Several lay friends came to live around; and Lord Arundel, Mr. David Lewis, Mrs. and Miss Bowden, may be called the nursing fathers and mothers of the infant Congregation. Before this time a site in Bayswater had been offered to the Oratorians, by whom, however, it was declined, and it was afterwards to be the site of the Oblate Fathers' Church of St. Charles Borromeo and the home of Henry Edward Manning.

But no one had forgotten that for the town, and not for the country, was St. Philip's rule designed; and now Bishop Wiseman wrote to Father Newman asking him to come to London to found an Oratory there. Newman had already thought of Birmingham, and the Pope's Brief mentioned Birmingham as the place of his foundation. This, of course, could have been altered; but it formed a sufficient reason, in Newman's opinion, for his refusal of Wiseman's invitation. Sir Robert Walpole spoke with some experience when he told his son that three-fourths of the chronicles of the period were lies not worth reading. Certainly great events have, at all times, been controlled by little incidents seemingly beneath the notice of pompous records: the "Go it, Ned!" scrawled in the corner of that despatch of the Duke of Clarence's, which decided the Battle of Navarino, but is not found in the Blue Books; the chance wound which led Ignatius of Loyola to take up the "Lives of the Saints" as better than nothing in his boredom; the passing of Gibbon when Vespers were being sung by monks by the Temple of Jupiter at Rome; the drowsiness of Ministers at a Richmond dinner while the Duke of Newcastle read the despatch to Lord Raglan determining the invasion of the Crimea; the badly-cooked chop which Napoleon said lost him Leipsic: all the innumerable littlenesses which make up the domestic side of history. Newman's settling at Birmingham has been assigned to solemn causes: by some to his desire to hide himself; by others to the desire of his new authorities that he should be hidden. O what a clatter of chatter if he had gone, as the Jesuit proposed, to Timbuctoo! We have heard enough about the seclusion in Birmingham of this apostle for whom, in truth, fine society had no fascinations, of this man of letters who hated to be interrupted in his literary moods. And, after all, perhaps the determining reason was a substantial one—the weight of his books. These had been carted to Maryvale at an incredible expense—a sum equal to nearly half of a year's income:—in his most flourishing Oxford days never exceeding £500. He had been moved to Cotton Hall from Maryvale and from his books; not greatly liking the separation. They were a sort of magnet to him, and, as he could get to them more easily and less expensively than they to him—to them he went.

A house in Alcester Street, Birmingham, was taken, therefore, into which he entered in January, 1849. His first work was to draw up, with the help of those about him, lists of names of the Fathers who should be at Birmingham, and of the Fathers who should be ceded to London. At last the approved list was sent to Cotton Hall to Faber, with a draft of the scheme for the foundation of the London Oratory, of which Faber was named the head. How it was formed, how it has flourished exceedingly, going from King William Street to South Kensington, needs not to be told here. Stanton and Dalgairns, late of Littlemore, were among those put on the London foundation; Bowles and St. John were among those who remained at Birmingham. Father Newman preached, on the opening day of the London Oratory, his sermon on the "Prospects of the Catholic Missioner." In 1850 he released the London Community from their obedience, and gave them "Home Rule," a system under which they have grown to be the very centre of London's spiritual activity—far surpassing the parent Oratory in the glory of stone and marble, and in the size and splendour of their appointments. Father Newman stayed at the Oratory in King William Street in 1852, for the Achilli trial; a time of excitement, during which he remained day and night, almost without interruption, before the Tabernacle. After his elevation to the Cardinalate he addressed the Brothers of the Little Oratory in their church at Brompton—strangers being also admitted—one Sunday afternoon, memorable to me as the only time I heard him preach—simple sentences said conversationally, then "flashes of silence," then sentences and pauses ringing the changes until the end. On other occasions of his visits to London he stayed with Lord Coleridge, with the Duke of Norfolk in St. James's Square, and with "Carissime" Church at the Deanery of St. Paul's.

The house in Alcester Street was poor enough, and the church adjoining was an old gin warehouse. "British spirits, pass this way," was the legend painted on an old iron door at the back of the altar. To a recent writer in a Birmingham newspaper, who went to Alcester Street in those days, and "saw John Henry Newman addressing a mere handful—sometimes, perhaps, a couple of hundred—of poor people, many of them Irish labourers," it appeared that "Rome had lost the skill with which she is credited of using with the greatest effectiveness every instrument at her command We happened to hear a discourse of his in those days in which there was a brilliant sketch of Napoleon and his influence on the national and religious life of Europe. It was delivered on a week-night, and the congregation, if we can trust to memory, did not consist of more than forty people, most of whom must have been very ill-educated." Newman himself, not "Rome," judged differently, however;

THE CHURCH OF THE LONDON ORATORY.

nor did he hesitate, when cholera broke out at Walsall—doubtless also among "poor people" and "mostly Irish" [O, qualifying English journalist!]—to put his life at their disposal; taking, with Father St. John, the place of the priest already prostrated by his labours.

Meanwhile, the man of letters was not idle. The "Discourses to Mixed Congregations" were issued from this house. The lectures on "Difficulties felt by Anglicans" were here composed, as were also the lectures on "The Present Position of Catholics in England," works in which his style attained its high-water mark. The lectures on the "Position of Catholics" were delivered in the Birmingham Corn Exchange, the lecturer, who wore his habit, remaining seated and reading from his MS. Admission was by ticket and one ticket was held at the first lecture by "Mr. Manning, late Archdeacon." At the end of the course of nine lectures, Bishop Ullathorne thanked the lecturer, who made, in reply, a singular confession: "It is a curious thing for me to say that, though I am of mature age, and have been very busy in many ways, yet this is the first time in my life that I have ever received any praise." Beyond this hall the lectures were heard—and praised, too. George Eliot read them "with great amusement (!)"—the mark of exclamation her own—"they are full of clever satire and description." All this time he was writing letters, and by them doing missionary work beyond the confines of his "poor people," "mostly Irish." English clergymen like Mr. Allies, and Scotch gentlemen like Mr. Hope-Scott, were writing for, and getting, help and guidance, previous to their reception into the Apostolic Church.

CHAPTER V.

AT THE ORATORY, EDGBASTON.

Mr. Spooner takes fright—The Building of the Oratory—The Daily Life—An Interval at Dublin—The Oratory School—Newman as a Talker—The literary work of the period—The Cardinalate—" Home " after Rome—Rednal—The last Resting-place.

IT was in 1852 that the Oratorians left Alcester Street for Edgbaston, where they have since remained. The plans for the house were drawn up by an engineer, Mr. Terence Flannagan, a cousin of one of the Fathers. During the building, some of the Littlemore stories were again in the air; and Father Newman had to explain his kitchen arrangements to the world:

UNDERGROUND CELLS.

May 15th, 1851.

Sir,—The *Times* newspaper has just been brought me, and I see in it a report of Mr. Spooner's speech on the Religious Houses Bill. A passage in it runs as follows : " It was not usual for the coroner to hold an inquest, unless when a rumour had got abroad that there was a necessity for one; and how was a rumour to come from the underground cells of convents? Yes, he repeated, underground cells; and he would tell honourable members something about such places. At this moment, in the parish of Edgbaston, within the Borough of Birmingham, there was a large convent of some kind or other being erected, and the whole of the underground was fitted up with cells !" The house alluded to in this extract is the one I am building for the Congregation of the Oratory of St. Philip Neri, of which I am Superior. The underground cells to which Mr. Spooner refers have been devised in order to economise space for offices commonly attached to a large house. I think they are five in number, but cannot be certain. They run under the kitchen and its neighbourhood. One is to be a larder, another is to be a coal-hole, beer, perhaps wine, may occupy a third.

At the Oratory, Edgbaston.

As to the rest, Mr. Spooner ought to know that we have had ideas of baking and brewing; but I cannot pledge myself to him that such will be their ultimate destination. Larger subterraneans commonly run under gentlemen's houses in London, but I have never in thought or word connected them with practices of cruelty and with inquests, and never asked their owners what use they made of them. When is this inquisition into the private matters of Catholics to end?

Your obedient servant,
JOHN HENRY NEWMAN.

The church was merely four brick walls, requiring no design beyond that of the local builder. So it has since remained, with the addition of the sanctuary, planned by Mr. J. H. Pollen. The place has been described by a man who has at least the qualifications of being familiar with every corner of it. He says:

About a mile and a-half from either of the Birmingham railway stations a visitor who passes along the whole length of Broad Street to the "Five Ways," and then turns up the Hagley Road, in the pleasant suburb of Edgbaston, reaches a plain, substantial red brick building on the right, which covers a very considerable piece of ground. It has no pretension to ecclesiastical style. The building adjoining, which has somewhat the appearance of a riding-school, and comes right up to the pavement with an almost unbroken red brick frontage of some eighty feet, is the big room of the Oratory School in which the well-known Latin Plays are annually performed; and an ostentatiously plain door at the nearer end of it, open in the morning and evening, leads to the Oratory Church, through a pleasing little round-arched cloister, which bears marks rather of ingenious contrivance than of any boldly conceived design. The church itself will probably disappoint the visitor, as it is small and dingy and without any architectural feature of interest, being, in fact, only a temporary building that has undergone alteration from time to time. The careful observer may, however, find in odd corners a bit of mosaic or of marble work that will please him; but where imitative decorations mainly prevail, the lover of the genuine is apt to distrust everything. The plain, oaken pulpit is that occupied at irregular intervals by Dr. Newman until two or three years ago; and up a passage behind a statue of St. Joseph will be found the small and dark chapel of "Bona Mors," where he daily said Mass at seven in the morning, until his elevation to the Sacred College gave him the privilege of doing so in his own private room. On the spectator's left of the high altar is the Cardinal's throne, where, unless indisposed, he presides at the chief ceremony on the great festivals of the Church, and notably at the High Mass on the Feast of St. Philip Neri (May 26th) and on that of the Immaculate Conception (December 8th).

.The Achilli case, and the damages for "libel" (such the Court of Queen's Bench held it to be)* on the apostate priest who provoked the notice of Newman by delivering anti-Popery lectures in Birmingham, may, perhaps, partly account for the poverty and inadequacy of the Oratory Church at Birmingham. It had been in the Cardinal's thoughts to build a worthy church, one which would in miniature recall St. Mark's, at Venice, the church he most of all admired; and M. Viollet le Duc came to Birmingham and prepared plans, which still exist, and which ought now at last to be turned to stone. But the Achilli trial timed with the entrance of the Fathers into the new house at Edgbaston; and Newman used to say that he had not the heart to ask for aid to build a big church after the inflowing of subscriptions to defray his legal expenses. Heavy as these were, there was a surplus of money subscribed; to be re-spent partly in Ireland, which had given, as usual, abundantly out of its own poverty.

There, at Edgbaston, for thirty-eight years, he lived, laboured, and loved. The little break made, early in the time, by his residence in Dublin as Rector of the Irish Catholic University, hardly destroys the continuity of that long spell of peaceful years. He was still "the Father" in his experimental absence; an experiment which did not succeed. Nor did he in Ireland cut himself off from old friends. The men of the Oxford Movement he gathered about him, his own converts, some of them: Mr. Allies, who has told the story of his momentous "Life's Decision"; Mr. Aubrey de Vere, the link between the vitalising of poetry by Wordsworth and Tennyson —his friends—and the vitalising of religion by Newman and Manning—himself a sharer alike in the literary and in the religious glory; Henry Bedford, who once well compared plain Father Newman to Napoleon, wearing no star among his generals who wore—constellations; J. H. Pollen, formerly a clergyman, and

* The *Times*, speaking of the result of the trial, said : "To Protestants and Romanists, the case, truly viewed, is unimportant ; its real significance is in the discredit it has tended to throw on our administration of justice, and the impression which it has tended to disseminate—that where religious differences come into play, a jury is the echo of popular feeling, instead of being the expositor of its own." A quarter of a century later a point in the case was quoted in one of the Courts as a precedent, when the following dialogue took place :—Lord Chief Justice COCKBURN : The case referred to created a painful impression on my mind, which can never be effaced.—The SOLICITOR-GENERAL : Your Lordship was counsel in it.—The LORD CHIEF JUSTICE : I was beaten, Mr. Solicitor ; and I ought to have been the victor.

always a fine *dilettante* in the arts; Le Page Renouf, the first of scholars in phases of Biblical history—now of the British Museum; Thomas Arnold, the son of Dr. Arnold and the brother of Matthew; Robert Ornsby, the biographer of Hope-Scott; Penny, who had been a visitor at Littlemore after his resignation of his living and his reception, before Newman's, into the Church; and W. H. Anderdon, who afterwards as a Jesuit Father fulfilled his apostolate, or continues it from Heaven. The lectures on "University Education" were delivered in Dublin; and the fame and name of Newman still inhabit the city from which he retired, at the end of 1859, with the conviction that he had served "a country which had tokens in her of an important future, and the promise of still greater works than she has yet achieved in the cause of the Catholic faith." Be it so!

Dublin or Oxford dwelt, for a time, in Newman's thoughts, as alternative places for an attempt to establish a College of high aims for Catholics. Dublin fell through, and the Oxford attempt was never made; for it failed, for good or for ill, to win the final approval of Pius IX., though Cardinals and others, including many fathers of sons, awaited its accomplishment with hopes and blessings. The Oratory School, established at Birmingham in 1859, supplied a smaller need, but supplied it well. One "Old Boy," Mr. Arthur Pollen, recalls:

At the Oratory we saw a good deal of the Cardinal; and, although he took no active share in the administration of the school, his interest in it was always great. Nothing pleased him more than making friends with the boys, and the many opportunities we had of personal contact with him made the friendship a real one. Of course, to us he was the greatest of heroes. Slight and bent with age, with head thrust forward, and a quick firm gait, the great Oratorian might often be seen going from corridor to corridor, or across the school grounds. His head was large, the pink biretta made it seem still more so, and he carried it as if the neck were not strong enough for the weight. His face changed but little; yet he would be a bold man who attempted to describe its sweetness, its firmness, and its strength. A pontifical ring and red sash and biretta were the only symbols of his rank; and no one living in the Oratory would imagine that it was the home of a Prince of the Holy Roman Church. It had been his special desire from the beginning that no ceremony or state should be maintained. He was always known by those in the house as "the Father"; and except in the part he took in the ceremonies of the Church, his dignity made small difference to his life. In the Latin Plays which he had prepared for the boys to act he always took the keenest interest, insisting on the careful rendering of favourite passages, and himself giving hints in cases of histrionic difficulty. In the school chapel he from time to time appeared, giving a short address, and assisting at the afternoon service. It is curious that it should have been in connexion with these two widely different occupations that we should have seen most of him. It is, perhaps, characteristic of his disposition, in which playfulness and piety were so sweetly combined.

Another "Old Boy," Dr. Sparrow, also remembers some of the methods and moods of his master:

The first boy to arrive was the eldest son of Serjeant Bellasis—R. G. Bellasis, who afterwards joined the Congregation of the Oratory, and is now Father Richard Bellasis, of the Birmingham Oratory. I went myself to the Oratory in 1863, and for eleven years enjoyed the privilege and blessing of the Cardinal's training. In those early days of the school we saw more of the Father (as we called him) than was possible for the students to have done in later years, owing to his age and physical weakness. Every month, in my time, each form went up to the Father's room and was examined by him *vivâ voce* in the work done during the preceding month, a trying ordeal for those who were nervous or idle, notwithstanding the kindness and gentleness of the Father, who was one of the most considerate and sympathetic of examiners. The Father always attached great importance to the "lesson by heart," and insisted on perfect accuracy and readiness in its repetition. He was always most particular to urge upon the boys a higher standard of honour, and never would tolerate anything mean or shabby. At the end of each term every boy went to the Father for what we called his "character," that is, the Father spoke to him privately as to his progress and behaviour during the past term. There was a story that in the early days of the school the Father received about the same time a letter from A., who had a boy at the school, complaining that the vacation was too long, and a letter from B., who also had a son at the school, complaining that the vacation was too short; Dr. Newman quietly (after cutting off the signatures) sent A.'s letter to B., and B.'s letter to A., after which no more was heard from either on the subject. When I was reading for the London University Intermediate Examinations in Arts along with another, the Father took us himself in classics and English literature, and I shall never forget those lectures, especially those in literature. He told us how greatly he admired Sir Walter Scott's novels; he also expressed a great liking for the "Rejected Addresses" as some of the cleverest parodies he had read; and he encouraged us to read good novels.

The life of the Fathers of the Oratory differs little from that of any group of secular priests living in community. A visitor to Edgbaston in the early 'eighties, Mr. C. Kegan Paul, gives the following account of the domestic routine:

Each Father has his own comfortable room,* library and bedroom in one, the bed within a screen, the crucifix above, and the prized personal little fittings on the walls. The library is full of valuable books, many of them once the private property of Dr. Newman, now forming the nucleus of a stately collection for the use of the Community. The quiet men who share this home come and go about their several businesses—the care of the school, whose buildings join, but are separate from the Oratory proper, the work in the church, in hearing confessions, saying Masses, and preaching. In the house the long soutane and biretta are worn; to go abroad they wear the usual dress of the clergy in England. Perhaps it is the dinner-hour, and the silent figures pass along the galleries to the refectory, a lofty room with many small tables, and a pulpit at one end opposite the tables. At one of these sits the Superior alone, clad like the rest save the red lines of his biretta, which mark his Cardinal's rank. But among his children, and in his home, he is still more the Superior and the Father than a Prince of the Church. At a table near him may, perhaps, be a guest, and at others the members of the Community, two and two. The meal is served by two of the Fathers, who take this office in turn; and it is only of late that Dr. Newman has himself ceased to take his part in this brotherly service, owing to his advanced years. During the meal a novice reads from the pulpit a chapter of the Bible, then a short passage from the life of St. Philip Neri, and then from some book, religious or secular, of general interest. The silence is otherwise unbroken save for the words needful in serving the meal. Towards the end, one of the Fathers proposes two questions for discussion, or rather for utterance of opinion. On one day there was a point of Biblical criticism proposed, and one of ecclesiastical etiquette (if the word may be allowed); whether, if a priest, called in haste to administer Extreme Unction, did so inadvertently with the sacred oil set apart for another purpose, instead of that for Unction, the act was gravely irregular. Each gave his opinion on one or other of these questions, the Cardinal on the first, gravely, and in well-chosen words. Yet it seemed to the observer that, while he, no doubt, recognised that such a point must be decided and might have its importance, there was a certain impatience in the manner in which he passed by the ritual question and fastened on that proposed from Scripture. After this short religious exercise, the company passed into another room for a frugal dessert and glass of wine, since the day chanced to be a feast; and there was much to remind an Oxford man of an Oxford Common-room, the excellent talk sometimes to be heard there, and the dignified unbending for a while from serious thought.

As a talker in the old days Newman has been described by Mr. J. A. Froude:

Newman's mind was world-wide. He was interested in everything

* "The Father," however, had two rooms allotted to him.

which was going on in science, in politics, in literature. Nothing was too large for him, nothing too trivial, if it threw light upon the central question, what man really was, and what was his destiny. His natural temperament was bright and light; his senses, even the commonest, were exceptionally delicate. He could admire enthusiastically any greatness of action and character, however remote the sphere of it from his own. Gurwood's "Despatches of the Duke of Wellington" came out just then. Newman had been reading the book, and a friend asked him what he thought of it. "Think?" he said, "it makes one burn to have been a soldier!" He seemed always to be better informed on common topics of conversation than anyone else who was present. He was never condescending with us (undergraduates), never didactic or authoritative; but what he said carried conviction along with it. Perhaps his supreme merit as a talker was that he never tried to be witty or to say striking things. Ironical he could be, but not ill-natured. Not a malicious anecdote was ever heard from him. Prosy he could not be. He was lightness itself—the lightness of elastic strength—and he was interesting because he never talked for talking's sake, but because he had something real to say.

At Littlemore he had told his young men to drop the *Mister*. "Call me Newman," he said. But, on this point, they were not bold enough to obey. "The Vicar" was a good get-out of the difficulty then, as "The Father" was at the Oratory, where he called the others by their Christian names — "William" and "John;" so that a title is not always the useless "tin-kettle" which Lord Strangford found his own. Archdeacon George Anthony Denison speaks of the Oriel Common-room in 1828, attended by "Whately, Arnold, Blanco White, Keble, Newman, Hampden," and others, as being "as dull a place socially as I can remember anywhere"—"there was no freedom of intercourse." But Mozley, also a Fellow, supposes the Archdeacon must have forgotten all about Oriel, since he jumbles together names of men he can never have seen together there.* Probably, Newman and his intimates did not unbosom themselves to Denison; possibly, Newman received some of his statements with even that withering "Really!" after hearing which, you were supposed to go and hide yourself. Certain it is that

* In fact, "G. A. D." never forgave Oriel the *hot* rhubarb tart served one day by the College cook, whom he had up and scolded for his ignorance of the tables of the great, where rhubarb was always served *cold!* "His eldest brother had just married a daughter of the Duke of Rutland, which was, of course, a great lift for a family of Leeds clothiers. No doubt dukes eat their rhubarb tart cold."—*T. Mozley.*

Newman told him in later years that "he was sorry for instances of harshness" towards him during their time at Oriel. Denison answered that he had no recollection of any such instances, but, if such there were, it must have been that Newman was far more in earnest than he. Newman, then and afterwards, was never wanting in tact as a talker. Father Bertrand Wilberforce, O.P., writes to me: "A characteristic story used to be told by my dearest father.* When Newman was Fellow of Oriel, during the Hampden† controversy, an American professor visited Oxford and dined at the high table. As the Fellows took different views in the controversy, it was never mentioned at dinner. The American, not understanding this, suddenly cried out: 'Well, Mr. Newman, what about this Hampden controversy?' Newman at once seized a spoon, and taking a potato from the dish, said: 'A hot potato?' Another time, when a naval chaplain was embarrassed by being asked whether his service on board ship was "High" or "Low," Newman interposed: "Surely that depends upon the tide." His own peculiar method of turning off questions which were not timely is well known. "Serious complications in Rome, Father," said Lord Edward Howard,‡ a member of Parliament anxious to get at Newman's mind during a crisis of the Roman question. "Yes," said the Father, quickly adding: "And in China." And there was something in his manner, we suppose, which prevented his questioners on such occasions from feeling that they were being trifled with. When he knew words would be wasted, he would not spend them. One of those about him having resolved to leave him, under circumstances likely to raise exclamations and to invite remonstrance, told him his determination. "By what train?" was all he said in acceptance of the painful inevitable. His offer to the Protestant champion, who challenged him to a discussion, that he would play him on

* Henry Wilberforce, who resigned the living of East Farleigh to become a Catholic, and to whom Newman dedicated "Callista": "To you alone, who have known me so long, and who love me so well, could I venture to offer a trifle such as this. But you will recognise the author in his work and take pleasure in the recognition." It is Henry Wilberforce who forms the most charming and human figure in all the group of Newman's contemporaries sketched by Mr. Mozley.

It was Hampden, by the way, who gave the nickname "Newmania" to Tractarianism.

‡ Afterwards first Lord Howard of Glossop, whom Newman came to London purposely to see upon his death-bed.

the violin, was another instance of his economy of words. Many were the visitors from afar who sought out the Father at the Oratory: strangers and wayfarers, generally in anxiety about their souls; old friends, too, some of whom, like Lord Emly and Aubrey de Vere, made a point of paying him a yearly visit. There, when both were bowed with age, met the two great Cardinals —the friends, counterparts and contrasts during sixty years. In the 'eighties they had half-an-hour together in Birmingham: saying not much, but looking each at each, with what self-revelations, what leave-takings! When the news of death came from Birmingham, the Prince of the Church at Westminster— though eight years younger—bowed his head, and said he felt he had his own notice to quit. Some went to the Oratory, as it were by night. Other business brought them to the Midlands: politics for example. The last time Mr. Gladstone visited the house, the invalid could not see him; but the politician, hearing that the Cardinal's arrangements for reading when reclining were defective, supplied a remedy. And there were some who were not even as Nicodemus; who were drawn to the Oratory, but never went. "I envy you your opportunity of seeing and hearing Newman," wrote George Eliot to Miss Hennell; "and I should like to make an expedition to Birmingham with that sole end." If only she had gone!

It was the "Apologia," written at Edgbaston in 1864, that did much more than confute Kingsley—it "breathed new life into me," said George Eliot, who, so speaking, spoke too for others. "Pray mark," she writes, "that beautiful passage in which he thanks his friend, Ambrose St. John. I know hardly anything that delights me more than such evidence of sweet brotherly love being a reality in the world." In 1866 he wrote at Birmingham his answer to Dr. Pusey's "Eirenicon:" "There was one of old time who wreathed his sword in myrtle; excuse me, you discharge your olive-branch as if from a catapult." In 1870 the "Grammar of Assent," was published; and five years later he issued his "Letter to the Duke of Norfolk on Mr. Gladstone's Expostulations": taking this very welcome opportunity for linking his name with that of one of the Old Boys of the Oratory School who was dear to him. Perhaps the life of the man of letters at Edgbaston was a more even one than it had ever been elsewhere: bringing with it no great discoveries, or fears, or surprises. He did not again "see a ghost," such as he had encountered in 1839, when the history of the fifth century revealed to him that the old Monophysite heresy was a type of Anglicanism; and such as reappeared to him in 1842 while translating Athanasius. He did not laugh to himself any longer as he had laughed at Maryvale over his composition of "Loss and Gain"—with its peculiar convert-clerical irony. He did not feel again the thrill of pleasure which ran through him as he took down the volumes of the Fathers from the shelves at Littlemore, after he had been received into the Church, and said, "You are mine now, you are mine now:" this nearest approach to almost bridal joy and sense of possession and triumph at last after long wooing, experienced by the lonely student, who had felt himself called to lead a single life from his youth, and for whom pleasure held out no temptations. Perhaps the most disturbing event of the Edgbaston period was the publication in the *Standard* of the private letter he had written—with a pen primed with panic, the pen of a recluse—during the sittings of the Vatican Council, to Bishop Ullathorne—between whom and himself the relations were always affectionate. And it "took away his breath" to find, one morning in 1885, among his letters one from Frank Power's sister, to say that she possessed a relic from Khartoum—a copy of "The Dream of Gerontius," given to her brother by Gordon, and scored by Gordon with incisive pencil marks at such passages as "Now that the hour is come, my fear is fled," and "Pray for me, O my friends." This poem, in which penetrating sincerity of feeling on a great subject finds the most poetical expression attained by Newman, was sent by him, in the first instance, to a periodical, the editor of which asked him for something: "I have routed this out of a drawer."

From Birmingham he had now and again to make a profession of Faith. When he had been nineteen years a Catholic, he declared:

I have been in perfect peace and contentment—I have never had one doubt. I was not conscious on my conversion of any inward difference of thought or of temper from what I had before. I was not conscious of firmer faith in the fundamental truths of revelation, or of more self-command; I had not more fervour; but it was like coming into port after a rough sea; and my happiness on that score remains to this day without interruption.

This was too mild a kind of announcement for some who still thought Newman might regret Anglicanism—showing by such thoughts at least their love of him, if also their ignorance of the Catholic Church. They needed a more defiant note, such as he struck when he said:

I have not had one moment's wavering of trust in the Catholic

CARDINAL NEWMAN.

Roughly sketched from the Portrait by Sir John Millais, R.A.

Church ever since I was received into her fold. I hold, and ever have held, a supreme satisfaction in her worship, discipline, and teaching; and an eager longing, and a hope against hope, that the many dear friends whom I have left in Protestantism may be partakers in my happiness. And I do hereby profess that Protestantism is the dreariest of possible religions; that the thought of the Anglican service makes me shiver, and the thought of the Thirty-nine Articles makes me shudder. Return to the Church of England! No! "The net is broken, and we are delivered." I should be a consummate fool (to use a mild term) if, in my old age, I left "the land flowing with milk and honey" for the city of confusion and the house of bondage.

He was only sixty-one, and had still a third of his life to run when he was writing thus of his "old age." The first letter I ever had from him, written early in 1874, ends: "Don't forget in your prayers that I am very old now, and need every help I can get from friends." For twenty years there were such closing passages and postscripts to letters addressed alike to friend and casual correspondent, postscripts always penetrating. By 1887 it had got to "Excuse a short letter—but I do not write without pain"; and the signature became as much as he could easily attempt at the end of the text indited in a hand rather freer than his own, but closely formed upon it, by his faithful friend and devoted other-self, Father William Neville.*

The news of his impending elevation to the Cardinalate reached Newman at the Oratory early in 1879 by rumour; and in March a letter from Cardinal Manning, giving an all but official message to that effect from the Pope, put an end to the "suspense" he said he felt while the news seemed to be known to everybody, but to him had never been formally announced. His was not the attitude of St. Bonaventura, who looked up from washing dishes in the kitchen to tell the Pope's messengers to hang up the hat in the passage. It was no bauble to Newman, whose respect for authority was the mainspring of his Anglican as of his Catholic life, and gave a value, in his eyes, to a recognition from the Father of Christendom. It was a seal set upon his fidelity by Leo XIII., who was wont to refer to him affectionately as "my Cardinal." It closed controversies which, while they lasted, had been sometimes hot, and always disturbing; vexed questions about an Oratorian establishment at Oxford; about the opportuneness of the Vatican Council's definition; about the dogmatism of Dr. Ward and the *Dublin Review*; about his general, but strictly conditioned, sympathy with the

* One of the six Anglican clergymen connected with St. Saviour's, Leeds, received into the Church together by Father Newman in 1851.

writers in the suppressed *Rambler*: the story of which suppression has yet to be frankly and calmly told. It was a pledge of goodwill from a quarter which, by rewarding him so highly, practically imposed silence on the old opponents. "They are all on my side now," said the aged Cardinal with a smile: a smile which had no poor human triumphing in it, but an added indulgent sweetness. Pusey did not quite understand how much it meant, when he wrote to Newman to congratulate him on his having the offer of the Cardinalate, and on his having, as rumour alleged, refused it. Writing later, Pusey said: "His still life in the Oratory at Birmingham had been an ideal to me. However, dear Newman thought that it would have been ungrateful in him towards those who had been at the pains to obtain this honour for him, and he accepted it, though he himself preferred obscurity. . . . Nothing has or can come between my deep love for John Henry Newman." In truth the old "still life in the Oratory" was not broken, once the new Cardinal had been in Rome and received his hat—choosing *Cor ad cor loquitur* as his motto, and St. George in Velabro as his titular church. It was the same still life, and the old retiring John Henry Newman; but it was the life crowned with the only glory he sought, the approbation of the living Church: a glory which, like the "harrowing praise" in Coventry Patmore's "Odes," humbles even while it exalts.*

Back to Birmingham he came, after weariness in Rome, in July, 1879. "To come home again!" he said to the flock who gathered to meet him—"in that word home how much is included. I know well that there is a more heroic life than a home life. We know St. Paul's touching words in which he says he is an outcast. We know, too, that Our Blessed Lord had not where to lay His head. But the idea of home is consecrated to us by St. Philip, who made it the very essence of his religious institute. Therefore I do indeed feel pleasure in coming home again." A few visits of a few days' duration through the ten remaining and declining years were the only absences from Edgbaston, except

* Dr. Döllinger, who, during his last years, gave up to gossip a mind meant for history, said that Newman's elevation showed that "his real views are not known at Rome," cheaply adding that "several of his works, had he written in French, Italian, or Latin, would have found a place on the 'Index.'" This opinion was printed and shown to Newman, who wrote: "It has pained me very much as manifesting a soreness and want of kindness for me which I did not at all suppose he felt. It makes one smile to suppose that Romans, of all men in the world, are wanting in acuteness, or that there are not quite enough men in the world who would be ready to convict me of heterodoxy if they could."

the stays at Rednal—the country-house of the Oratorians.

The end came at last quickly. There had been little illnesses; and the failure of strength was so apparent that it seemed as if a breath or a movement would extinguish the faint spark. On one of these days he asked some of the Fathers to come in and play or sing to him Father Faber's hymn of "The Eternal Years." When they had done so once, he made them repeat it, and this several times. "Many people," he said, "speak well of my 'Lead, kindly Light,' but this is far more beautiful. Mine is of a soul in darkness—this of the eternal light." Into that light he wakened up on Monday evening, the 11th of August, 1890, in the ninetieth year of his age.

There at Rednal he was laid to rest by loving hands. His grave he shares with Ambrose St. John, who died in 1875, and in whose memory Newman planted the now spreading bed of St. John's wort down one side of the small enclosure. They loved each other in life; and in death they are not divided. On either side is a grave—that of Father Edward Caswall, who died in 1878, and that of Father J. Gordon, who died in 1853. Two other graves are there: that of Robert Boland, who died while a novice; and that of a son of Father Pope—an Oratorian after the death of his wife. Thus do tender human relationships cling—as is fitting in presence of the ashes of that human heart—to the graveyard where Cardinal Newman lies. Even the dust of a woman is in that last resting-place of celibacy: Frances Wootten, widow of the Oxford doctor I have mentioned as attending the inmates of the monastery at Littlemore; she who had followed Newman, first into the Church, and then to Birmingham to be the Matron, the Vice-Mother, at the Oratory School. And my last words shall leave him in this association with women. He, who gave himself to none, belonged to all; becoming the tender father and helper to many of that sex which intimately enters into the life of even a St. Paul by Damaris, of a St. Francis of Sales by Madame de Chantal. Among the flowers sent to that last resting-place were two wreaths, one of which bore the name of a woman who offered it "to the most dear memory of Cardinal Newman, who has been benefactor, guide, and counsellor through life." Another garland came from the Baroness Burdett-Coutts, as "a tribute of respect to a great Englishman, whose beauty of life shed its light of purity over his own century, but belongs to all ages:" a legacy that shall endure, by time untarnished and undimmed by death.

FAC-SIMILE COPY OF "LEAD, KINDLY LIGHT."

Lead, Kindly light, amid the encircling gloom
    Lead Thou me on!
The night is dark, and I am far from home —
    Lead Thou me on!
Keep Thou my feet; I do not ask to see
The distant scene — one step enough for me.

I was not ever thus, nor prayed that Thou
    Shouldst lead me on.
I loved to choose and see my path, but now
    Lead Thou me on!
I loved the garish day, and, spite of fears,
Pride ruled my will: remember not past years.

So long Thy power hath blest me, sure it still
    Will lead me on,
O'er moor and fen, o'er crag and torrent, till
    The night is gone;
And with the morn those angel faces smile
Which I have loved long since, and lost awhile.

                John Newman

Transcribed
for Dr F. G. Lee
Oct. 28. 1872

APPENDIX.

THE MAN OF LETTERS.

On his Conversion—The Vatican Council—"I said something Sharp"—About a borrowed Book—On his Essay on the "Development of Christian Doctrine"—On the Achilli Case—"The Glorious St. Denis"—About a "Broad" Bishop of London—"Above all a Disciple of the Church"—"Not at all the case that I left the Anglican Church from despair"—"My dear old First College"—On his being made a Cardinal—"I cannot be well till I am back"—"Such a Son"—The Birmingham Free Library—"Proselytising"—The Oath as a Parliamentary test—The "Jesuit in Disguise" Theory.

CARDINAL NEWMAN, who was a ruler in the larger things of Literature, was careful and deliberate in his composition of little things. No other man in a private position wrote so many letters which have been preserved. When he began the "Tracts for the Times," he began also a correspondence on a large scale with the readers of the Tracts seeking aid or offering adhesion; and these letters were lesser Tracts—a part of the apostolate to which he had consecrated his pen. They were as neatly written as they were carefully composed; and, just as they moulded the style of innumerable letters from other hands, so, too, the very penmanship in which they were indited has been reproduced by admirers, widely different in temperament, but yielding alike to the same subtle influence of discipleship even in the framing of an A or an X. Of the early letters—those written during the first and Anglican half of the Cardinal's career—a large number were returned to the writer, who outlived nearly all his early correspondents; and by him they were handed, during his lifetime, to the sister of his two brothers-in-law, Thomas and John Mozley, to be edited by her after the manner of her editing of the letters of her other brother, the

Rev. Dr. James Mozley. One of these letters, and one of the last he wrote in this series, has been destroyed: committed to the flames by an Anglican clergyman, to whom Pusey sent it to get the guilty thing out of sight, and who seemed as though he would annul the act of secession by burning the record of it. To many friends, the Hermit of Littlemore wrote in October, 1845, announcing that he was returning to the Old Religion; but to Dr. Pusey, his comrade-in-arms, he wrote perhaps with more emotion than to any.

ON HIS CONVERSION.
To the Rev. Dr. Pusey.

Littlemore, October 8th, 1845.

My dearest Pusey,—This will not go till all is over. This night I am expecting Father Dominic, the Passionist, who is on his way from Aston, in Staffordshire, to Belgium, to attend a Chapter.

I trust he will receive me, Bowles, and Stanton into what I believe to be the one and only fold of the Redeemer. I do not expect it will take place till Friday.

Ever yours, my dear Pusey, most affectionately,

J. H. N.

On the back of this letter Dr. Pusey wrote the following words:

Tu autem, Domine, miserere nobis.

E. B. P.

Kyrie eleëson,
Christe eleëson,
Kyrie eleëson.

This is almost the exact counterpart of the letter written to Keble, which Keble walked about with all day at Hursley not daring to open it, knowing intuitively what tidings it told.

THE letters written by Cardinal Newman during the other and Catholic half of his life, discriminating hands will assort and select for publication. While thanking friends who have offered me private correspondence for use here, I defer to Father Neville's desire that such letters, at least in the first instance, should be communicated to him, as the Cardinal's literary legatee. But I permit myself to gather together in handy form a group of letters appearing in scattered places, which supplement and complete the collection of public Letters of Cardinal Newman's Catholic Life, already issued in handy form, and possessed by most of my present readers. It has been hinted by a writer in the *Times*—and Mr. J. A. Froude is a writer in the *Times*—that the Fathers of the Birmingham Oratory are not fit persons to be entrusted with the task of editing Cardinal Newman's letters; and Mr. Froude is believed to be not unwilling to undertake it in their stead. He, at least, would suppress nothing for edification's sake: but how can he trust the Oratorians? Let this ex-disciple assure himself that if he ransacked the portfolios of his former master, and the portfolios of his friends, he would find nothing of shame, no littleness to show how unheroic are the best of men: he could not, if he would, practise on Cardinal Newman what he practised on Carlyle. There is perhaps one letter which some of Cardinal Newman's friends wish he had not written; and this because it might easily be misunderstood unless taken in context with the temper of the time at which it was composed—a temper happily evanescent. Write it he did, however; and now that his private letters, as well as those he formally published, belong to history, I answer the challenge of the *Times* by reprinting the letter he addressed to his Bishop during the sittings of the Vatican Council. The *Standard* correspondent it was who obtained a copy of the letter; and the first hint he publicly gave of its contents was the occasion of two letters to the *Standard*, which may here be prefixed to the most impulsive, and the most confidential, letter Newman ever wrote.

THE VATICAN COUNCIL.

To the Editor of the Standard.

The Oratory, March 15th, 1870.

Sir,—I am led to send you these few lines in consequence of the introduction of my name, in yesterday's *Standard*, into your report of the "Progress of the Œcumenical Council." I thank you for the courteous terms in which you have, on various occasions, as on the present, spoken of me; but I am bound to disavow what you have yesterday imputed to me, viz., that I have "written to my Bishop at Rome, Dr. Ullathorne, stigmatising the promoters of Papal Infallibility as an insolent, aggressive faction."

That I deeply deplore the policy, the spirit, the measures of various persons, lay and ecclesiastical, who are urging the definition of that theological opinion, I have neither intention nor wish to deny, just the contrary. But, on the other hand, I have a firm belief, and have had all along, that a Greater Power than that of any man or set of men will overrule the deliberations of the Council to the determination of Catholic and Apostolic truth, and that what its Fathers eventually proclaim with one voice will be the Word of God.

I am Sir, your obedient servant,

JOHN H. NEWMAN.

To the Editor of the Standard.

March 22nd, 1870.

Sir,—In answer to the letter of "The Writer of the Progress of the Council," I am obliged to say that he is right and I am wrong as to my using the words "insolent and aggressive faction" in a letter which I wrote to Bishop Ullathorne. I write to make my apologies to him for contradicting him. I kept the rough copy of this private letter of mine to the Bishop, and on reading the writer's original statement I referred to it and did not find there the words in question.

This morning a friend has written to tell me that there are copies of the letter in London, and that the words certainly are in it. On this I have looked at my copy a second time, and I must confess that I have found them. I can only account for my not seeing them the first time by my very strong impression that I had not used them in my letter, confidential as it was, and from the circumstance that the rough copy is badly written and interlined. I learn this morning from Rome that Dr. Ullathorne was no party to its circulation. I will only add that when I spoke of a faction I neither meant that great body of Bishops who are said to be in favour of the definition of the doctrine, nor any ecclesiastical Order or Society external to the Council. As to the Jesuits, I wish distinctly to state that I have all along separated them in my mind, as a body, from the movement which I so much deplore. What I meant by a faction, as the letter itself shows, was a collection of persons drawn together from various ranks and conditions in the Church.

I am, Sir, your obedient servant,

JOHN H. NEWMAN.

A fortnight later the *Standard* published the letter itself, and here it is:

To the Bishop of Birmingham.

Rome ought to be a name to lighten the heart at all times, and a Council's proper office is, when some great heresy or other evil impends, to inspire hope and confidence in the Faithful; but now we have the greatest meeting which ever has been seen, and that at Rome, infusing into us by the accredited organs of Rome and of its partisans (such as the *Civiltà*, the *Armonia*, the *Univers*, and the *Tablet*) little else than fear and dismay. When we are all at rest and have no doubts, and—at least practically, not to say doctrinally—hold the Holy Father to be infallible, suddenly there is thunder in the clear sky, and we are told to prepare for something, we know not what, to try our faith, we know not how. No impending danger is to be averted, but a great difficulty is to be created. Is this the proper work of an Œcumenical Council?

As to myself personally, please God, I do not expect any trial at all; but I cannot help suffering with the many souls who are suffering, and I look with anxiety at the prospect of having to defend decisions which may not be difficult to my own private judgment, but may be most difficult to maintain logically in the face of historical facts. What have we done to be treated as the Faithful never were treated before? When has a definition *de fide* been a luxury of devotion and not a stern painful necessity? Why should an aggressive, insolent faction be allowed "to make the heart of the just sad, whom the Lord hath not made sorrowful"? Why cannot we be let alone when we have pursued peace and thought no evil?

I assure you, my Lord, some of the truest minds are driven one way and another, and do not know where to rest their feet—one day determining "to give up all theology as a bad job," and recklessly to believe henceforth almost that the Pope is impeccable; at another, tempted to "believe all the worst which a book like 'Janus' says;" others "doubting about the capacity possessed by Bishops drawn from all corners of the earth to judge what is fitting for European society," and then, again, angry with the Holy See for listening to the "flattery of a clique of Jesuits, Redemptorists, and converts." Then, again, think of the store of Pontifical scandals in the history of eighteen centuries which have partly been poured forth and partly are still to come. What Murphy inflicted upon us in one way M. de Veuillot is indirectly bringing on us in another. And then, again, the blight which is following upon the multitude of Anglican Ritualists, etc., who themselves perhaps —at least their leaders—may never become Catholics, but who are leavening the various English denominations and parties (far beyond their own range) with principles and sentiments tending towards their ultimate absorption into the Catholic Church.

With these thoughts ever before me, I am continually asking myself whether I ought not to make my feelings public, but all I do is to pray those early Doctors of the Church whose intercession would decide the matter—Augustine, Ambrose, and Jerome, Athanasius, Chrysostom, and Basil—to avert the great calamity. If it is God's will that the Pope's infallibility is defined, then is it God's will to throw back "the times and moments" of that triumph which he has destined for His kingdom, and I shall feel I have but to bow my head to His adorable, inscrutable Providence.

Nowhere more than in this letter does Cardinal Newman illustrate the claim he once made—that he "always thought for others more than for himself." There were times, however, when another rule was necessary, when he had to speak out, perhaps painfully to individuals, to have the truth heard at all. The following frank betrayal of his occasional methods as a writer is a key to the letters he wrote with a seeming asperity smiting with his pen as with a sword :

"I SAID SOMETHING SHARP."
To the Rev. Sir William Cope, Bart.*

The Oratory, February 13th, 1875.

My dear Sir William,—The death of Mr. Kingsley, so premature, shocked me. I never from the first have felt any anger towards him. As I said in the first pages of my "Apologia," it is very difficult to be angry with a man one has never seen. A casual reader would think my language denoted anger, but it did not. I have ever felt from experience that no one would believe me in earnest if I spoke calmly. When again and again I denied the repeated report that I was on the point of coming back to the Church of England, I have uniformly found that if I simply denied it, this only made newspapers repeat the report more confidently; but if I said something sharp, they abused me for scurrility against the Church I had left, but they believed me. Rightly or wrongly, this was the reason why I felt it would not do to be tame and not to show indignation at Mr. Kingsley's charges. Within the last few years I have been obliged to adopt a similar course towards those who said I could not receive the Vatican Decrees. I sent a sharp letter to the *Guardian*, and, of course, the *Guardian* called me names, but it believed me, and did not allow the offence of its correspondent to be repeated.

As to Mr. Kingsley, much less could I feel any resentment against him, when he was accidentally the instrument, in the good Providence of God, by whom I had an opportunity given me, which otherwise I should not have had, of vindicating my character and conduct in my "Apologia." I heard, too, a few years back from a friend that he chanced to go into Chester Cathedral, and found Mr. Kingsley preaching about me kindly, though, of course, with criticisms on me. And it has rejoiced me to observe lately that he was defending the Athanasian Creed, and, as it seemed to me, in his views generally, nearing the Catholic view

---

* Sir William Cope, to whom this letter was addressed a few days after Mr. Kingsley's death, but to whom the Cardinal had before expressed the same views in conversation, was one of the Anglican clergymen present at the obsequies of the Cardinal in the Birmingham Oratory. Sir William forms a fitting link between the two men who may be called in different senses the authors of the "Apologia," for he inherited Bramshill when the grooms and trainers of his predecessor were objects of special interest to Kingsley at the neighbouring parsonage of Eversley.

of things. I have always hoped that by good luck I might meet him, feeling sure there would be no embarrassment on my part, and I said Mass for his soul as soon as I heard of his death.

Most truly yours,
JOHN H. NEWMAN.

On this revelation of his need on occasions to use words in excess of his own sentiment, so that he might get a hearing at all, much remains to be said. Only one comment, of many comments suggesting themselves, need here be made. While still in charge of the University pulpit, he was accused of "Romanising" the Church of England. A soft denial turned away no wrath. So one day he fell into rhetoric, and now we know the reason. Speaking of those who might be led to Rome, and making himself hypothetically one of these straying sheep, he said : "We shall find too late that we are in the arms of a pitiless and unnatural relative, who will but triumph in the arts which have inveigled us within her reach, for in truth, she is a Church beside herself—crafty, obstinate, wilful, malicious, cruel ; unnatural as madmen are, or, rather, she may be said to resemble a demoniac, possessed with principles, thoughts, and tendencies not her own." After that, who could say he was going to Rome ?—until he went ! The following letters can be printed without any further explanation than they themselves afford, or than is supplied by headlines or by a few necessary notes. They are given in the order of their date :

ABOUT A BORROWED BOOK.
To the Rev. Dr. Greenhill.[*]

Ushaw, Durham, January 13th, 1846.

Dear Greenhill,—I am much obliged to you for your thoughtfulness about the volume of St. F. de Sales. I do not want it at this moment, but by the end of this month, I think, I should like to have it for the purpose of packing. You would have been quite right to direct to me "Revd." Thank you for your consideration.

Very truly yours,
JOHN H. NEWMAN.

[*] Dr. Greenhill says of this : "His note was written in answer to one which I sent to him very shortly after he left the Anglican Church, about returning a volume of St. François de Sales which he had lent me. I directed my note to 'J. H. Newman, Esq.,' with an apology for my mistake, if I had done wrong. We have lately been amused at reading W. G. Ward's joking threat to call Dean Goulburn 'E. M. Goulburn, Esq.,' if he (Goulburn) persisted in addressing him as 'the Rev. W. G. Ward' ; so that the way in which Newman replied to my apology is interesting."

ON HIS ESSAY ON THE "DEVELOPMENT OF CHRISTIAN DOCTRINE."

To the Bishop of La Rochelle.

The Oratory, Birmingham, February, 1850.

Monseigneur,—It is with deep emotion that I have read the letter addressed by your Lordship to M. Jules Gondon on my book. It shows no less than the two articles signed by your Lordship in the *Ami de la Religion*, such kindness and indulgence as fills me with the liveliest gratitude. You have deigned to put yourself in the place of the author when he wrote his work, sympathising with his difficulties, and making allowance for them in your appreciation of his labours.

As far as the success of the book is concerned, I am in no ways anxious, leaving everything in God's hands. If it be His will to make use of the hypothesis of development and to turn it to the defence of His Church, I shall never cease to praise His holy name. If, on the other hand, He sees it is not available for His glory, I bow, without regret, to His supreme will. In either case, never shall I recall to mind the favourable manner in which you have judged my work without feeling the most tender, the deepest gratitude. Besides, when I reflect upon the political struggles in which your country is at this moment engaged, it is impossible for me not to be struck by your condescension, nor to estimate still more highly this precious mark of your kind favour.

It is from the bottom of my heart that I submit what I have written to the judgment of the Church. When I composed my work I had not the happiness of being of the number of her children. The book, therefore, is but a mere essay; it does but enter upon a subject scarcely mooted up to our days, and of such extreme delicacy that one hardly dare handle it. I cannot, then, but be thankful to those who are good enough to point out to me any portions of my work which appear to them ambiguous. But when dignity of rank, superiority of intellect, and acknowledged sanctity are united in the person who deigns to take notice of my essay, unthankful indeed should I be were I to refuse him the tribute of my gratitude and lasting attachment. Be pleased, my Lord, to receive my very sincere thanks for the encouragement you have bestowed upon me by the two indulgent criticisms you have passed upon my work.

Your Lordship's very humble servant,

JOHN H. NEWMAN, Congr. Orat.

ON THE ACHILLI CASE.

To the Revv. Fathers Bryan and Synon.*

Edgbaston, November 11th, 1852.

My dear Rev. Brothers and Friends, — Your most kind and welcome letter and its enclosure have come to me to-day, almost on the eve of my being brought up to judgment on the matter to which it relates. I lose not a moment in returning to you my most respectful and heartfelt thanks to your excellent Bishop, to the clergy, and to your good Catholics throughout the Diocese of Limerick, rich and poor, who have taken part in so noble an act of Christian charity. You say well when you speak of the high value of such an act "to my feelings, even independent of the consideration of the amount contributed." It is, indeed, the sympathy of Catholics, as shown in such contributions—the certainty of their goodwill and love—the conscientiousness of their prayers for me, which has been my great earthly consolation in a considerable trial.

Hence it has happened that as the proceedings in which that trial consisted have become more and more oppressive, they have, to my own feelings, become less and less painful, for I have been supported, month after month, by a more intense force of Catholic sympathy up to this date. And now when (after the fashion of those in past times, with whom I am not fit to be mentioned in one breath) I am to be called before a judgment seat, I know I carry with me into Court ten thousand Catholic hearts, and I have no anxiety, no distress, no fear of any kind as to what will befall me. Yet, while I say this I cannot allow you in your kindness to make light of the value of your great gift, considered in itself. It is most affecting to me. I feel it at once most cruel, yet a great honour, that I should call forth such lavish offerings from so impoverished a people; and, moreover, it is a call upon my warmest gratitude, viewed merely as a large sum contributed to my necessities, for unless you and other Catholics had come forward in my behalf, what was in store for me for the rest of my life but an enormous weight of debt, of which I had not the means of discharging the twentieth part?

Pray accept my best thanks yourselves for consenting to be the medium of the bounty of Limerick, and for all the trouble you have taken in the matter from first to last. Begging your good Bishop's blessing, and the prayers of yourselves and all who have been so charitable towards me,

I am, my dear Rev. Brethren,
Very sincerely yours in Christ,
JOHN H. NEWMAN.

* Acknowledging £312 as contribution of the Diocese of Limerick to the expenses of the Achilli trial.

"THE GLORIOUS ST. DENIS."
To the Editor of the Univers

The Oratory, Birmingham, St. Denis's Day, 1852.

My dear M. Gondon,—It is seven years ago this day since I was received into the Catholic Church, and on the occasion of this anniversary I beg of you personally to express my most hearty and respectful thanks to the Catholics of France, to their Lord Bishops, to their zealous priests, to the numerous persons of distinction, as well as to those of the humblest rank, for the generous donations which they have sent to me, on account of the unexpected charges which weigh on me. I cannot call these charges a misfortune, when they have procured for me an honour of such a peculiar character as the sympathy and generosity of a Catholic nation. The manifestation of which my embarrassments have been the cause is, on the part of France, an act of liberality worthy of the most zealous, the most active, and the most friendly of Catholic countries.

The only unworthy person in all this affair is he who receives these testimonials of kindness. I am surprised at seeing myself the object of such sympathies; and I think I may without presumption believe that the glorious St. Denis, who presided over my reception into the bosom of Catholicism, has, as it were, presented me a second time to the embraces of the Church, by recommending me to the tender charity of the great nation of which he is the apostle. Confiding in your kindness to offer my homage to their Eminences the Cardinals, and their Lordships the Bishops, and to the other good and generous persons to whom I owe so much, I beg of you to accept yourself, as well as all your colleagues of the *Univers*, my heartiest thanks.

I am, my dear M. Gondon,
Your sincere friend and servant in Jesus Christ,
JOHN H. NEWMAN.

ABOUT A "BROAD" BISHOP OF LONDON.
To the Rev. H. T. Ellacombe.†

The Oratory, January 21st, 1870.

My dear Ellacombe,—You must have thought me very unkind in not answering you sooner, but I have been cruelly occupied, and indeed am now. You must, and I hope will, take this as my apology. I do not know your Bishop, and am not sure that he is an easy man to know. I do not at all wonder at your great anxiety about him. He

---

* Acknowledging the first instalment of subscriptions towards the expenses of the Achilli trial.

† Who, like many other people, was distressed at the appointment of Bishop Temple to the See of Exeter in 1870, and took counsel of Newman.

may, however, be one of those who dislike what, when I was young, R. Wilberforce and H. Froude used to call "180 degree sermons," that is, sermons which were resolved to bring in the whole circuit of theology in the space of twenty minutes.

We used to think it was the great fault of Evangelicals—that they would not let religious topics come in naturally, but accused a man of not being sound in religion if he dared to speak of sanctification without justification, regeneration, etc., etc. Now it may be that Dr. Temple has a way of preaching on the immediate subject which is before him, and lets other topics take their chance. At the same time I grant that grace is not a subject which he ought to leave out on the occasions you mention. On the whole, if I may venture to speak on the subject, I think it wise, as well as kind, to give him a fair trial, and not to expect evil from him. There is no doubt he has many very high qualities. I do not like to think he would deny the necessity of Divine grace, and I should trust you will find him saying all he ought to say when he is actually upon the subject. It will concern me very much to find you disappointed.

Thank you for your kind greetings for the New Year, and, though very late now, I hope you will let the heartiness with which I return them make up for the tardiness.

Very sincerely yours,
JOHN H. NEWMAN.

"ABOVE ALL A DISCIPLE OF THE CHURCH."
To Monsignor Darboy, Archbishop of Paris.*

1870.

The doctrine of infallibility has now been more than sufficiently promulgated. Personally I have never had a shadow of doubt that the very essence of religion is protection from error, for a revelation which could stultify itself would be no revelation at all. I have always inclined to the notion that a General Council was the magisterial exponent of the creed, just as the Judges of England are the legal expounders of the statutes of our realm. Unfortunately, a General Council may be hampered and hindered by the action of infidel Governments upon a weak or time-serving Episcopate. It is therefore better that the individual command of Christ to Peter to teach the nations and to guard the Christian structure of society should be committed to his undoubted successor. By this means there will be no more of those misunderstandings out of which Jansenism and Gallicanism have arisen, and which in these latter days have begotten here in

---

* Who gave it, not long before his imprisonment and death at the hands of the Communists, to the late Monsignor Rogerson, formerly British Catholic chaplain at Paris.

England the so-called Branch Theory, by which the Catholic-minded members of a Protestant Church claim the blessings of Catholicism. When Rome spoke on this subject every misgiving vanished; for, if by some fiction those who love me will have it that I am a teacher of the Faithful, I am above all a disciple of the Church, *doctor fidelium discipulus ecclesiae.*

I am, with reverence and affection,
Your devoted and humble servant,
JOHN HENRY NEWMAN.

"NOT AT ALL THE CASE THAT I LEFT THE ANGLICAN CHURCH FROM DESPAIR."

To Mrs. H———n.*

The Oratory, July 3rd, 1871.

My dear Mrs. H———,—As to your question, suggested by your friends, it is not at all the case that I left the Anglican Church from despair—but for two reasons concurrent, as I have stated in my "Apologia"—first, which I felt *before* any strong action had been taken against the Tracts or me, namely, in 1839, that the Anglican Church *now* was in the position of the Arian Churches of the fourth century, and the Monophysite Churches of the fifth, and this was such a shock to me that I at once made arrangements for giving up the editorship of the *British Critic*, and in no long time I contemplated giving up St. Mary's. This shock was the *cause* of my writing No. 90, which excited so much commotion. No. 90, which roused the Protestant world against me, most likely never would have been written except for this shock.

Thus you see my condemnation of the Anglican Church arose *not* out of despair, but, when everything was hopeful, *out of my study of the Fathers.* Then, as to the second cause, it began in the autumn of 1841, six months after No. 90, when the Bishops began to charge against me. This brought home to me that *I had no business in the Anglican Church.* It was not that I despaired of the Anglican Church, but that their opposition *confirmed* the interpretation which I had put upon the Fathers, that they **who loved** the Fathers could have no place in the Church of England. As to your further question, whether, *if I* had stayed in the Anglican Church *till now*, I should have joined the Catholic Church at all, at any time now or hereafter, I think that most probably I should *not;* but, observe, for this reason, because God gives grace, and if it is not accepted He withdraws His grace; and since, of His free mercy, and from no merits of mine, He then offered me the grace of conversion, if I had not acted upon it, it was to be

* A lady who was shortly afterwards received into the Church by the Cardinal.

expected that I should be left, a worthless stump, to cumber the ground and to remain where I was till I died.

Of course, you are endlessly bewildered by hearing and reading on both sides. What I should recommend you, if you ask me, is to put aside all controversy, and close your ears to advocates on both sides for two months, and not to open any controversial book, but to pray God to enlighten you continually, and then at the end of the time to find where you are. I think, if you thus let yourself alone, or rather take care that others let you alone, you will at the end of the time see that you ought to be a Catholic. And if this is the case, it will be your duty at once to act upon this conviction. But if you go on reading, talking, being talked to, you will never have peace. God bless you, and keep you, and guide you, and bring you safe into port.

Yours most sincerely,
JOHN H. NEWMAN.

"YOUR SHRINKING BACK IS VERY NATURAL."

To the same.

The Oratory, May 6th, 1872.

My dear Mrs. H——,—I sincerely rejoice and thank God that you are so far advanced by His mercy as to be convinced that the Church in communion with Rome is that which Christ set up in the beginning as the Oracle of Truth and the Ark of Salvation. He who has led you thus far will lead you on still, into her fold, and into full faith and peace.

Your shrinking back is very natural, and does but show that you realise what you are doing. I felt it most painfully myself when I was approaching the Church. I said, "How do I know but that, as soon as ever I become a Catholic, my eyes will be opened, and I shall see I have taken a false and wrong step?" But I never have had even a temptation for one instant to think I acted wrongly. It has been as contrary to every thought, feeling, impulse, tendency of my mind, and has been so all along, to entertain such an idea, as it would be contrary to my nature to think of cutting my throat, or cheating a friend. I simply can't admit the idea into my mind. And my experience is that of a hundred others. I can but give my own testimony in answer to your apprehension. Then, again, I think those persons who do feel anxiety before they take the step are the very persons who are unlikely to feel misgivings afterwards. Further recollect the grace of God will not leave you without some great fault of yours; so that if you are courageous, as those heroes of romance who go resolutely forward, undismayed by the threatening aspects of their enemies, you will find the phantoms of evil which you fear will give way to you, and vanish into thin air.

As to your second difficulty, it is a very trying one, but is no argument for your acting against your conscience. God will support you under it, and it will not be so heavy a trial as you fear. With my best wishes and prayer,

   I am, my dear Mrs. H——, most truly yours,
                                   JOHN H. NEWMAN.

"MY DEAR OLD FIRST COLLEGE."
*To the Rev. Dr. Greenhill.**

                           The Oratory, January 6th, 1878.

My dear Dr. Greenhill,—I thank you for your most kind letters. It is a great gratification to me to be again a member of my dear old first college, and a second pleasure to find that gratification so understood and sympathised in on the part of my friends and of Trinity men, such as yourself.

I should have answered you before, on the receipt of your first card, but have been thrown into great confusion by the death of one of my dear friends in this House, whose burial had not yet taken place; also by the death of James Mozley, whose family is in great grief, and with whom I am connected.

Let me wish you all blessings of this sacred season, and assure you that

                                   I am, sincerely yours,
                                   JOHN H. NEWMAN.

ON HIS BEING MADE A CARDINAL.
To the Right Rev. Monsignor Gilbert, V.G.

                             The Oratory, March 22nd, 1879.

Very Rev. and dear Provost of Westminster,—I have delayed my reply to the most welcome congratulations addressed to me by yourself and the Canons of Westminster, on occasion of the singular honour which the Holy Father graciously intends for me, simply because I have been confused at receiving words so very kind and so very earnest. How can I refuse a praise which is so pleasant? How can I accept what, according to my knowledge of myself, is so beyond what I can justly claim?

However, such words at least are signs of your affectionate goodwill towards me, and no misgiving about myself can deprive me of a right to them. As such I thank you for them with all my heart and shall treasure them.

* Who had congratulated him on being made **Honorary Fellow of** Trinity **College,** Oxford.

It is, indeed, a happiness as great as it is rare that those special feelings which are commonly elicited in a man's friends after his death, should in my own case find expression in my behalf while I am yet alive.

With deep gratitude to those who have been so good to me,

I am, my dear Very Rev. Provost,

Sincerely yours in Christ,

JOHN H. NEWMAN.

"I CANNOT BE WELL TILL I AM BACK."

To Mr. W. S. Lilly.*

48, Via Sistina, Rome, May 10th, 1879.

My dear Lilly,—I got Father Pope to tell you that the £500, which you so thoughtfully sent, has been received, because I am so tired myself.

I am pulled down by a bad cold, which I really think would go if the bad weather went; but I am necessarily a prisoner to my bedroom and to my bed, and cannot speak or write without an effort. At Turin on Sunday I had to squeeze, kneeling at Mass, against a man who had a very bad cough, and I said to myself, "What if I catch it?" As we went down to Genoa, I said, "If I was at home, I know from my throat that something there would turn to a bad cold." When at Genoa I felt so uncomfortable that I said, "Let us rest at Pisa for two days," and so we did. Thence we got to Rome in a day, but by that time the cold and cough were fixed. I have seldom had so bad a one.

I have been a fortnight here, and have said just one Mass, and been into one church—St. Peter's! Is not this melancholy? The Holy Father has been abundantly kind, inquiring after me every day. My public days begin on Monday, and it seems as if I should not be able to go out up to then! There has been cold hail yesterday and to-day. I am much better, but very much pulled down. There is *no* fever on me; all I want is fine weather. The thought comes on me that I cannot be well till I am back. But perhaps when I once well turn the corner, all will come right.

Most truly yours,

JOHN H. NEWMAN.

* Who, as Secretary of the Catholic Union, had forwarded a sum subscribed by friends for the new Prince of the Church.

"SUCH A SON."

To the Hon. W. Towry Law.

The Oratory, January 29th, 1882.

My dear Mr. Law,—Thank you for your most interesting memorials of your son.* There is not a word too much in them, as you fear. It is a favour we are not often given to be able to follow, year by year, the formation of a saintly mind. How God has blessed you in giving you such a son! It is a consolation for much suffering, and a sort of pledge of other mercies yet to come.

Most truly yours,
JOHN H. CARD. NEWMAN.

THE BIRMINGHAM FREE LIBRARY.

To the Mayor of Birmingham.†

The Oratory, June 2nd, 1882.

Dear Mr. Mayor,—I do not think I can be wrong in asking you to be the channel of the contribution which I enclose to the Public Library Fund, but if I am taking an informal step I rely on your known zeal for its interests to excuse me. I have long wished to take a part, however small, in so great a work, but it is only within the last few weeks that to do so has been in my power.

I am, dear Mr. Mayor, your faithful servant,
JOHN H. CARD. NEWMAN.

"PROSELYTISING."

To Miss L——.‡

The Oratory, Birmingham, July 6th, 1882.

Dear Miss L——,—Your letter has interested me very much, and has led me to entertain great hopes that God is calling you by His grace into His Church; and, of course, it is your duty to attend to that call, and that you may duly attend to it I earnestly pray.

---

* Father Augustus Henry Law, S.J., died in 1880, on the Zambesi Mission, South Africa.

† Enclosing £20 towards the Library Fund.

‡ This young lady, in trouble about her soul, wrote to Cardinal Newman for advice; and thus innocently he answered her. But, under the flaunting title of "Proselytism," a Suffolk rector forwarded the Cardinal's letter to the *Times* as addressed to "a motherless schoolgirl of sixteen." No wonder the Jesuits had been expelled from France! for "This is not Christianity: this is not common humanity." O, the days of the Apostles—of the girl martyrs! To Canon Longman His Eminence wrote in this connexion:

So much I have no difficulty in saying; but when you come to the question what your duty is at this time, my answer is not so easy. I consider that a stranger to you cannot give you satisfactory advice. You should have recourse to some priest on the spot; put your whole case before him, and go by his judgment. The Father Jesuits, for instance, are sure to be careful and experienced priests, and they would, on talking to you, decide whether, young as you are, and dependent, I suppose, on your father, it would be advisable for you at once to undergo the great trial of breaking with him. Our Lord tells us "to count the cost." The change of religion is a most serious step, and must not be taken without great preparation by meditation and prayer.

Do not doubt that Our Lord will guide you, and happily, if you place yourself unreservedly in His hands.

Yours sincerely,
J. H. CARDINAL NEWMAN.

THE ABOLITION OF THE OATH AS A PARLIAMENTARY TEST.

To F. W. Chesson.

Birmingham, May 8th, 1883.

Dear Sir,—I do not know how to answer your question without using more words than I like to trouble you with. I feel myself to be so little of a judge on political or even social questions, and religious questions so seldom come before us, that I rarely feel it a duty to form and to express an opinion on any subject of a public nature.

I cannot consider the Affirmation Bill involves a religious principle; for, as I had occasion to observe in print more than thirty years ago, what the political and social world means by the word "God," is too often not the Christian God, the Jewish, or the Mohammedan, not a Personal God, but an unknown God, as little what Christians mean by God as the Fate, or Chance, or *Anima Mundi* of a Greek philosopher.*

"Few days pass without my having letters from strangers, young and old, men and women, on the subject of the Catholic religion. I answer them that it is the one and only true and safe religion. But as to the personal duty of the particular applicant, I decline to determine it at a distance, and advise him to address someone in his own neighbourhood. If I know of a priest who has experience of converts I name him. This, I have no doubt, is what I wrote in the cases which you bring before me."

* The following is the passage, taken from the "Discourses on the Scope and Nature of University Education," to which the Cardinal alludes: "I cannot take it for granted, I must have it brought home to me by tangible evidence, that the spirit of the age means by the Supreme Being what Catholics mean. Nay, it would be a relief to my mind to gain some ground of assurance that the parties influenced by that spirit had, I will not say a true apprehension of God, but even so much as the idea of what a true

Hence it as little concerns religion whether Mr. Bradlaugh swears by no God with the Government, or swears by an impersonal, or material, or abstract and ideal something or other, which is all that is secured to us by the Opposition. Neither Mr. Gladstone nor Sir Stafford Northcote excluded from Parliament what religion means by an "atheist."

Accordingly it is only half my meaning if I am made to say that I "do not approve, in any sense of the word, of the Affirmation Bill." I neither approve nor disapprove. I express no opinion upon it; and that, first because I do not commonly enter upon political questions, and next because, looking at the Bill on its own merits, I think nothing is lost to religion by its passing and nothing gained by its being rejected.

I am, dear Sir, your faithful servant,

JOHN H. CARD. NEWMAN.

THE "JESUIT IN DISGUISE" THEORY.

To the Editor of the Spectator.

Birmingham, May, 1883.

Sir,—You have for many years taken so kind an interest in me, that I venture to hope you will let me publish in your columns a few lines on a personal matter, which in no sense concerns the *Spectator*. Sir William Palmer,* with whom I was very intimate fifty years since, and who had so much to do with the start of what was called the "Oxford Movement," in an account of it which he has given in the May number of the *Contemporary Review*, writes about me as follows:

"[Hurrell] Froude had, with Newman, while travelling in Italy, been anxious to ascertain the terms upon which they could be admitted to communion by the Roman Church, supposing that some dispensation might be granted which would enable them to communicate with Rome without violation of conscience." Again, after saying that I considered myself "predestined," etc., he proceeds: "Those who conversed with him were not aware of this; nor did they know that while in Italy he had sought, in company with Froude, to ascertain the terms on which they might be admitted to communion with Rome, and had been surprised on learning that an acceptance of the decrees of the Council of Trent was a necessary preliminary. Had I been aware of these circumstances, I do not know whether I should have been able to co-operate so cordially as I did with this great man."

To this statement, namely, that I was party to an inquiry as to the apprehension is. Nothing is easier than to use the word, and mean nothing by it. The heathens used to say, 'God wills,' when they meant 'Fate'; 'God provides,' when they meant 'Chance'; 'God acts,' when they meant 'Instinct' or 'Sense'; and 'God is everywhere,' when they meant 'the Soul of Nature.'"

* Not to be confounded with Mr. William Palmer, of Magdalen, Lord Selborne's brother, who died a Catholic after coquetting with the Greek Church.

terms on which, by dispensation or otherwise, Hurrell Froude and I might be admitted to communion with Rome, I give an absolute and emphatic denial. The passage in Froude's "Remains," on which Sir William founds it, with the note appended by me as editor of its publication, runs as follows :

"Froude says, in a letter to a friend, 'The only thing I can put my hand on as an acquisition is having formed an acquaintance with a man of some influence at Rome, Monsignor [Wiseman], the head of the [English] College, who has enlightened [Newman] and me on the subject of our relations to the Church of Rome. We got introduced to him, to find out whether they would take us in on any terms to which we could twist our consciences, and we found to our dismay that not one step could be gained without swallowing the Council of Trent as a whole.'"

I added this note in protest :

"All this must not be taken literally, being in a jesting way of stating to a friend what really was the fact, viz., that he and another availed themselves of the opportunity of meeting a learned Romanist to ascertain the ultimate points at issue between the Churches."

As on the publication of the "Remains" I disclaimed by anticipation Sir William Palmer's present misstatement, so I repudiate it again now. One thing I thank him for, that, by publishing it in my lifetime, he has given me the opportunity of denying it.

I am, Sir, etc.,

JOHN H., CARDINAL NEWMAN.

www.ingramcontent.com/pod-product-compliance
Lightning Source LLC
Chambersburg PA
CBHW020329090426
42735CB00009B/1463